Civil Liberties

Other Books of Related Interest:

At Issue Series

Gay Marriage

Policing the Internet

Current Controversies Series

Assisted Suicide

Gays in the Military

Global Viewpoints Series

Human Trafficking

Workers' Rights

Introducing Issues with Opposing Viewpoints Series

Abortion

Banned Books

Labor Unions

Religion in Schools

Issues That Concern You Series

Child Labor

Opposing Viewpoints Series

Church and State

Interracial America

Judicial Activism

Civil Liberties

Noël Merino, Book Editor

GREENHAVEN PRESS
A part of Gale, Cengage Learning

Detroit • New York • San Francisco • New Haven, Conn • Waterville, Maine • London

Elizabeth Des Chenes, *Director, Publishing Solutions*

For more information, contact:
Greenhaven Press
27500 Drake Rd.
Farmington Hills, MI 48331-3535
Or you can visit our Internet site at gale.cengage.com

Articles in Greenhaven Press anthologies are often edited for length to meet page requirements. In addition, original titles of these works are changed to clearly present the main thesis and to explicitly indicate the author's opinion. Every effort is made to ensure that Greenhaven Press accurately reflects the original intent of the authors. Every effort has been made to trace the owners of copyrighted material.

LIBRARY OF CONGRESS CATALOGING-IN-PUBLICATION DATA

Civil Liberties / Noël Merino, book editor.
p. cm. -- (Global viewpoints)
Summary: "Civil Liberties: examines current, often controversial, topics of worldwide interest and importance from a variety of international perspectives"-- Provided by publisher.
Includes bibliographical references and index.
ISBN 978-0-7377-6261-7 (hardback) -- ISBN 978-0-7377-6437-6 (paperback)
1. Civil rights--Cross-cultural studies. I. Merino, Noël.
JC574.C54 2012
323--dc23

2012022607

Printed in the United States of America
1 2 3 4 5 16 15 14 13 12

Contents

Chapter 2: Media Freedom and Freedom of the Press

Chapter 3: The Right to Due Process

Chapter 4: The Right to Privacy

Foreword

> *"The problems of all of humanity can only be solved by all of humanity."*
> *—Swiss author Friedrich Dürrenmatt*

Global interdependence has become an undeniable reality. Mass media and technology have increased worldwide access to information and created a society of global citizens. Understanding and navigating this global community is a challenge, requiring a high degree of information literacy and a new level of learning sophistication.

Building on the success of its flagship series, Opposing Viewpoints, Greenhaven Press has created the Global Viewpoints series to examine a broad range of current, often controversial topics of worldwide importance from a variety of international perspectives. Providing students and other readers with the information they need to explore global connections and think critically about worldwide implications, each Global Viewpoints volume offers a panoramic view of a topic of widespread significance.

Drugs, famine, immigration—a broad, international treatment is essential to do justice to social, environmental, health, and political issues such as these. Junior high, high school, and early college students, as well as general readers, can all use Global Viewpoints anthologies to discern the complexities relating to each issue. Readers will be able to examine unique national perspectives while, at the same time, appreciating the interconnectedness that global priorities bring to all nations and cultures.

Material in each volume is selected from a diverse range of sources, including journals, magazines, newspapers, nonfiction books, speeches, government documents, pamphlets, organization newsletters, and position papers. Global Viewpoints is truly global, with material drawn primarily from international sources available in English and secondarily from US sources with extensive international coverage.

Features of each volume in the Global Viewpoints series include:

- An **annotated table of contents** that provides a brief summary of each essay in the volume, including the name of the country or area covered in the essay.
- An **introduction** specific to the volume topic.
- A **world map** to help readers locate the countries or areas covered in the essays.
- For each viewpoint, an **introduction** that contains notes about the author and source of the viewpoint explains why material from the specific country is being presented, summarizes the main points of the viewpoint, and offers three **guided reading questions** to aid in understanding and comprehension.
- **For further discussion** questions that promote critical thinking by asking the reader to compare and contrast aspects of the viewpoints or draw conclusions about perspectives and arguments.
- A worldwide list of **organizations to contact** for readers seeking additional information.
- A **periodical bibliography** for each chapter and a **bibliography of books** on the volume topic to aid in further research.
- A comprehensive **subject index** to offer access to people, places, events, and subjects cited in the text, with the countries covered in the viewpoints highlighted.

Global Viewpoints is designed for a broad spectrum of readers who want to learn more about current events, history, political science, government, international relations, economics, environmental science, world cultures, and sociology—students doing research for class assignments or debates, teachers and faculty seeking to supplement course materials, and others wanting to understand current issues better. By presenting how people in various countries perceive the root causes, current consequences, and proposed solutions to worldwide challenges, Global Viewpoints volumes offer readers opportunities to enhance their global awareness and their knowledge of cultures worldwide.

Introduction

> *"The indiscriminate use of the law against every activity or expression that some group dislikes is a route to the disappearance of freedom of expression altogether."*
>
> *—Martin Wolf, "Freedom of Speech Is a Right, but Self-Restraint Is a Virtue,"* Financial Times, *February 8, 2006*

The concept of civil liberties refers to a varied set of liberties seen as deserving of value and respect by social institutions. Civil liberties may or may not be protected by explicit law, and legal protection for civil liberties varies widely around the world. Civil liberties are freedoms; therefore, protection for the exercise of civil liberties generally involves noninterference by law and government except as necessary to protect the freedom. Some key civil liberties include freedom of expression, freedom of assembly, freedom of the press, freedom from arbitrary detention, and freedom from unwanted invasion of privacy. None of these freedoms are ever absolute, and the extent of justifiable limits on these freedoms is contentious and varies among countries and cultures. Looking at one particular controversy about freedom of expression helps to shed light on the widespread approaches to civil liberties throughout the world.

Freedom of expression is one of the most basic civil liberties, and it affects individuals, groups, and institutions such as the press. Having the freedom to express oneself through speech, action, and even silence, has always been one of the most important ways for people in civil society to protest certain government actions and to suggest different viewpoints.

One of the most common disputes in societies regarding freedom of expression occurs when a certain form of expression offends the religious sensibilities of a particular group. A highly publicized conflict of this sort occurred in 2005 in Denmark, with reverberations felt around the world. The Danish newspaper *Jyllands-Posten* published twelve editorial cartoons depicting the prophet Muhammad. These cartoons were reprinted in newspapers in several dozen other countries around the world. The cartoons were offensive to many Muslims for two reasons: most of the cartoons depicted an image of Muhammad, which for many Muslims is considered idolatry and is prohibited; and most of the cartoons were critical of Islam.

Anger about the cartoons led to attacks on the Danish embassies in Pakistan, Syria, Lebanon, and Iran. Angry protests were staged around the world. Death threats were made against the cartoonists, causing many to go into hiding. In the Middle East, a boycott against Danish goods was organized, costing Danish businesses over €100 million. Threats and attacks related to the cartoons continued in the years following. One cartoonist in particular, Kurt Westergaard, has repeatedly been the target of assassination attempts, including one at his home in 2010. Violence as a result of the incident caused at least two hundred deaths.

Jyllands-Posten's culture editor, Flemming Rose, defended the publication of the cartoons as a response to growing limits on free expression: "I commissioned the cartoons in response to several incidents of self-censorship in Europe caused by widening fears and feelings of intimidation in dealing with issues related to Islam." Rose argues that the idea that freedom of expression should be limited by the beliefs of religious people is not consistent with the principles of the modern democratic state: "If a believer demands that I, as a nonbeliever, observe his taboos in the public domain, he is not asking for my respect, but for my submission. And that is incompatible with a secular democracy." Furthermore, Rose claims that respect for freedom of expression actually furthers freedom of religious expression: "Nowhere do so many religions coexist peacefully as in a democracy where freedom of expression is a fundamental right. In Saudi Arabia, you can get arrested for wearing a cross or having a Bible in your suitcase, while Muslims in secular Denmark can have their own mosques, cemeteries, schools, and TV and radio stations."

Ironically, Rose's intention to challenge self-censorship by publishing the cartoons may have simply reinforced many people's desire to self-censor after seeing the damage done. More than four years after the original controversy, Yale University Press published a book about the incident, *The Cartoons That Shook the World*. Written by a Danish-born professor of politics in the United States, Jytte Klausen, the book recounts the event through the eyes of politicians in the Middle East, Muslim leaders in Europe, and the Danish editors and cartoonists. But Yale University Press made the decision not to print the actual cartoons because of fear of fallout. The author stated, "I agreed to the press's decision to not print the cartoons and other hitherto uncontroversial illustrations featuring images of the Muslim prophet, with sadness. But I also never intended the book to become another demonstration for or against the cartoons, and hope the book can still serve its intended purpose without illustrations."

Weighing the importance of various freedoms against other social needs is a subject of frequent debate in the realm of civil liberties. Governments often demand limits on freedom of the press when it comes to state secrets, but many governments want limits on media freedom for any criticism. The freedom to not be unfairly detained leads to the implementation of due process rules meant to protect this civil liberty. And yet, in the name of safety, law enforcement officials around the world detain suspects they believe pose a great danger before they have actually been convicted. The right to privacy would seem to, at minimum, apply within the four walls of one's home. But does surveillance in public violate this civil liberty, or does the social interest in safety and order take precedence? The different approaches to civil liberties such as these are explored through the diverse viewpoints in *Global Viewpoints: Civil Liberties.*

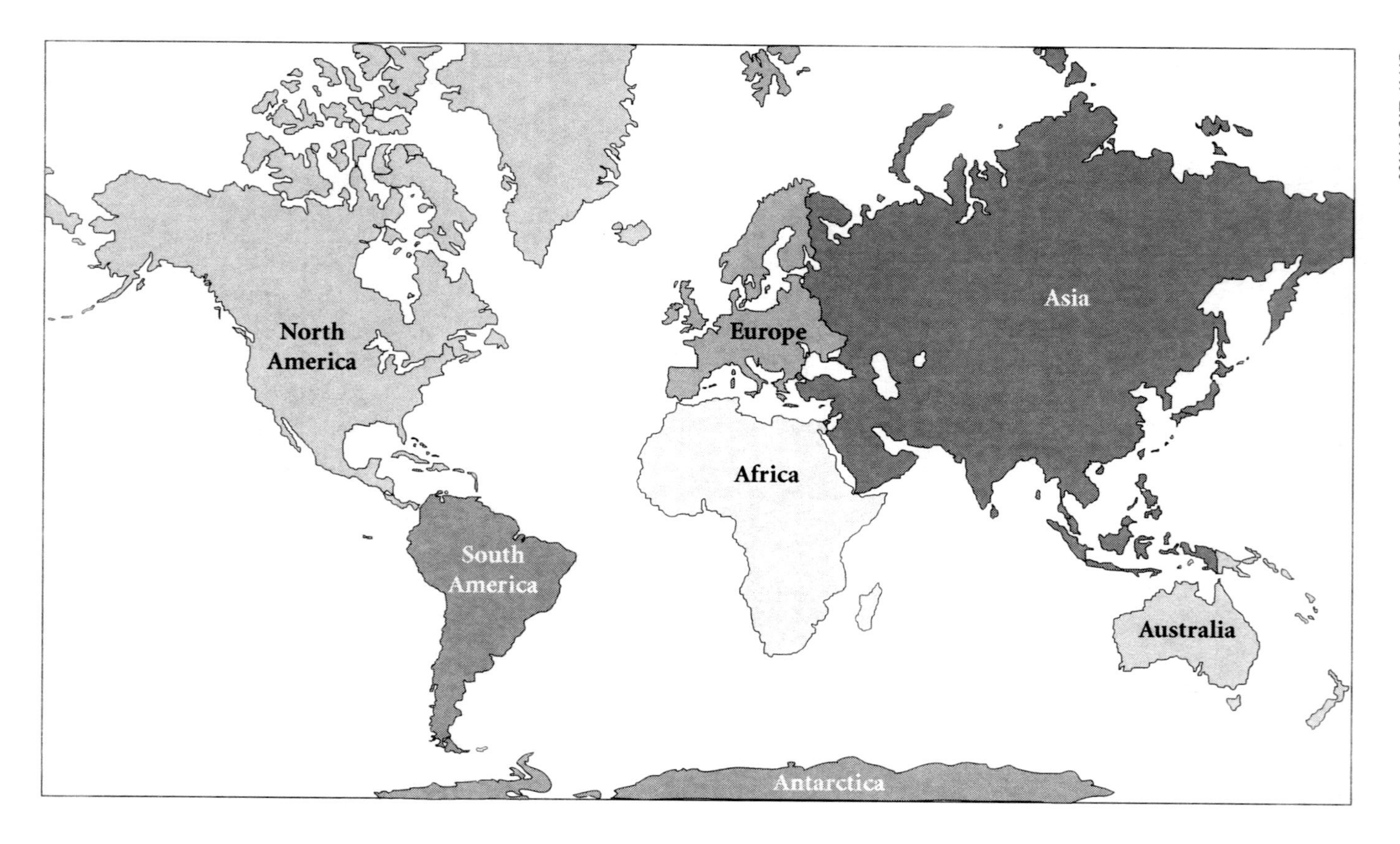
North America
Europe
Asia
Africa
South America
Australia
Antarctica

Free Speech and Freedom of Expression

VIEWPOINT 1

Free Speech in Western Countries Is Under Siege

Robert Skidelsky

In the following viewpoint, Robert Skidelsky argues that freedom of speech in the West is in danger. Skidelsky contends that there is a disturbing trend toward censoring historical inquiry and a pressure to engage only in politically correct speech. He concludes that the defense of free speech must be reaffirmed in order to maintain free society. Skidelsky is emeritus professor of political economy at the University of Warwick and writes a monthly column for Project Syndicate, titled Against the Current, which is syndicated in newspapers around the world.

As you read, consider the following questions:

1. According to the author, what are the two main traditional limitations on free speech under British law?
2. To what author does Skidelsky attribute the view that free inquiry is necessary to advance knowledge?
3. What example does Skidelsky give in support of his view that social phenomena have come to be neutrally labeled?

Recently, at a literary festival in Britain, I found myself on a panel discussing free speech. For liberals, free speech is a key index of freedom. Democracies stand for free speech; dictatorships suppress it.

Robert Skidelsky, "Free Speech Under Siege," Project Syndicate, June 21, 2011.

Freedom of Speech in the West

When we in the West look outward, this remains our view. We condemn governments that silence, imprison, and even kill writers and journalists. Reporters Sans Frontières [Reporters Without Borders] keeps a list: 24 journalists have been killed, and 148 imprisoned, just this year [2011]. Part of the promise we see in the "Arab Spring" is the liberation of the media from the dictator's grasp.

Yet freedom of speech in the West is under strain. Traditionally, British law imposed two main limitations on the "right to free speech." The first prohibited the use of words or expressions likely to disrupt public order; the second was the law against libel. There are good grounds for both—to preserve the peace and to protect individuals' reputations from lies. Most free societies accept such limits as reasonable.

But the law has recently become more restrictive. "Incitement to religious and racial hatred" and "incitement to hatred on the basis of sexual orientation" are now illegal in most European countries, independent of any threat to public order. The law has shifted from proscribing language likely to cause violence to prohibiting language intended to give offense.

A blatant example of this is the law against Holocaust denial. To deny or minimize the Holocaust is a crime in 15 European countries and Israel. It may be argued that the Holocaust was a crime so uniquely abhorrent as to qualify as a special case. But special cases have a habit of multiplying.

Freedom of speech in the West is under strain.

France has made it illegal to deny any "internationally recognized crimes against humanity." Whereas in Muslim countries it is illegal to call the Armenian massacres of 1915–1917 "genocide," in some Western countries it is illegal to say that they were not. Some east European countries specifically prohibit the denial of Communist "genocides."

The Censorship of Historical Inquiry

The censorship of memory, which we once fondly imagined to be the mark of dictatorship, is now a major growth industry in the "free" West. Indeed, official censorship is only the tip of an iceberg of *cultural* censorship. A public person must be on constant guard against causing offense, whether intentionally or not.

Breaking the cultural code damages a person's reputation, and perhaps one's career. Britain's Home Secretary Kenneth Clarke recently had to apologize for saying that some rapes were less serious than others, implying the need for legal discrimination. The parade of gaffes and subsequent groveling apologies has become a regular feature of public life.

In his classic essay "On Liberty," [British philosopher] John Stuart Mill defended free speech on the ground that free inquiry was necessary to advance knowledge. Restrictions on certain areas of historical inquiry are based on the opposite premise: The truth is known, and it is impious to question it. This is absurd; every historian knows that there is no such thing as final historical truth.

It is not the task of history to defend public order or morals, but to establish what happened. Legally protected history ensures that historians will play safe. To be sure, living by Mill's principle often requires protecting the rights of unsavory characters. David Irving writes mendacious history, but his prosecution and imprisonment in Austria for "Holocaust denial" would have horrified Mill.

The Pressure for Political Correctness

By contrast, the pressure for "political correctness" rests on the argument that the truth is unknowable. Statements about the human condition are essentially matters of opinion. Because a statement of opinion by some individuals is almost certain to offend others, and since such statements make no contribution to the discovery of truth, their degree of offensiveness be-

Of the Liberty of Thought and Discussion

If all mankind minus one were of one opinion, and only one person were of the contrary opinion, mankind would be no more justified in silencing that one person, than he, if he had the power, would be justified in silencing mankind. Were an opinion a personal possession of no value except to the owner; if to be obstructed in the enjoyment of it were simply a private injury, it would make some difference whether the injury was inflicted only on a few persons or on many. But the peculiar evil of silencing the expression of an opinion is, that it is robbing the human race; posterity as well as the existing generation; those who dissent from the opinion, still more than those who hold it. If the opinion is right, they are deprived of the opportunity of exchanging error for truth: if wrong, they lose, what is almost as great a benefit, the clearer perception and livelier impression of truth, produced by its collision with error.

John Stuart Mill, "On Liberty," 1859.

comes the sole criterion for judging their admissibility. Hence the taboo on certain words, phrases, and arguments that imply that certain individuals, groups, or practices are superior or inferior, normal or abnormal; hence the search for ever more neutral ways to label social phenomena, thereby draining language of its vigor and interest.

A classic example is the way that "family" has replaced "marriage" in public discourse, with the implication that all "lifestyles" are equally valuable, despite the fact that most people persist in wanting to get married. It has become taboo to describe homosexuality as a "perversion," though this was precisely the word used in the 1960s by the radical philosopher Herbert Marcuse (who was praising homosexuality as an expression of dissent). In today's atmosphere of what Marcuse would call "repressive tolerance," such language would be considered "stigmatizing."

The classic doctrine of free speech is in crisis.

The sociological imperative behind the spread of "political correctness" is the fact that we no longer live in patriarchal, hierarchical, monocultural societies, which exhibit general, if unreflective, agreement on basic values. The pathetic efforts to inculcate a common sense of "Britishness" or "Dutchness" in multicultural societies, however well intentioned, attest to the breakdown of a common identity.

Free Speech in Crisis

Public language has thus become the common currency of cultural exchange, and everyone is on notice to mind one's manners. The result is a multiplication of weasel words that chill political and moral debate, and that create a widening gap between public language and what many ordinary people think.

The defense of free speech is made no easier by the abuses of the popular press. We need free media to expose abuses of power. But investigative journalism becomes discredited when it is suborned to "expose" the private lives of the famous when no issue of public interest is involved. Entertaining gossip has mutated into an assault on privacy, with newspapers claiming that any attempt to keep them out of people's bedrooms is an assault on free speech.

You know that a doctrine is in trouble when not even those claiming to defend it understand what it means. By that standard, the classic doctrine of free speech is in crisis. We had better sort it out quickly—legally, morally, and culturally—if we are to retain a proper sense of what it means to live in a free society.

VIEWPOINT 2

No Country Should Declare Free Speech an Absolute Right

Yasmin Alibhai-Brown

In the following viewpoint, Yasmin Alibhai-Brown argues that it is a mistake to be fundamentalist about freedom of speech. Alibhai-Brown claims that it is easy to defend free speech in dramatic cases of censorship, but she cautions that there are legitimate limits on acceptable free speech. Furthermore, she contends that along with the freedom to express one's self is the freedom of others to react. Alibhai-Brown is a Ugandan-born British journalist and author, as well as a senior fellow at the Foreign Policy Centre in the United Kingdom.

As you read, consider the following questions:

1. According to Alibhai-Brown, what French author expressed an absolutist view about freedom of speech?
2. The author claims that parents stop their children from saying rude things for what reason?
3. What US Supreme Court justice does Alibhai-Brown quote as supporting limits on speech?

Too many states use brute force to quell and gag their people. In our Western democracies, governments withhold information, stop legitimate protest, control speech and

Yasmin Alibhai-Brown, "No Democracy Should Declare Free Speech an Absolute Right," *The Independent* (UK), April 11, 2011.

even thought. All wrong, must be resisted, agreed. Most of us, though, will not speak with one voice on the burning of the Koran by Sion Owens, a BNP [British National Party] candidate for the Welsh assembly. And what about the website that sells cheeky jihadi, al-Qa'ida baby T-shirts and maternity clothes? Tory MP [member of Parliament] Robert Halfon is apoplectic and wants the site closed down. Are you with or against him? Do we teach children that words can wound or that their entitlement to speak trumps everything else?

Freedom of Speech Fundamentalism

Freedom of speech is endlessly discombobulating and testing. In the unspoiled meadows of ideals or unbound skies of philosophical postulations, it is easy to be unequivocal. Some in the real world, too, are enviable absolutists who believe the slightest tremor of concern is a concession and invitation to authoritarianism. Their God is [French writer] Voltaire, who decreed that even when one hates what is being said by somebody, one must "fight to the death" for the right of that person to hold forth. (Noble rhetoric. Correct me if I am wrong, but I can't think of a single such martyr.)

A protracted and violent struggle against mental tyranny was fought by Europeans and today in the Arab lands citizens are inspired by the same emancipatory, human impulses. However, Voltaire's spiritual children can be fundamentalist, thoughtless and irrational, blind and deaf, unresponsive to the complexities of modern life, of individual and group psychology, inequality and power. Freedom of expression is not black and white, but a thousand shades of grey. Its meaning and practice need to be unpacked. Each situation demands exhaustive and exhausting analysis before informed positions can be arrived at.

I was on a panel at the Oxford Literary Festival last week [in April 2011] trying to do just that with journalist David Aaronovitch in the chair, and John Kampfner, chief executive of Index [on] Censorship, and the blogger Guido Fawkes, who has (inexplicably) become an unaccountable and scary political force. For Fawkes anything goes. Easy, though not for those he picks on. Kampfner is an indefatigable campaigner against legal and official curtailments, the use of money by the rich to enforce censorship through the courts and unjust control. I agree with him most of the time.

Freedom of expression is not black and white, but a thousand shades of grey.

Reaction to Expression and Speech

When the powerful come down heavy on citizens or communities and vigilantes do the same, they must be resisted. It is intolerable that artists are inhibited, imprisoned or killed as just was Juliano Mer-Khamis, the exceptional Jewish, Israeli-Palestinian actor and founder of the Freedom Theatre in Jenin. Members of Hamas are allegedly behind this barbarism. And here our very own local religious hoodlums have threatened to kill Usama Hasan, a lecturer and London imam, because he refuses to reject evolution.

Come away from dramatic confrontations and the law to more intractable conflicts. Then it gets awfully complicated. The web is a wonderful liberator but also a nameless, shameless sniper. Professional blogger [Lorelle] VanFossen rightly warns that when people express anything and everything, "... there are consequences, the right to react, that other freedom." That other freedom—disrespected by most libertarians. [American writer] Saul Bellow complained much about the closing down of public discussion in the US: "We can't open our mouths without being denounced as racists, misogynists, supremacists, imperialists or fascists." He blamed the media. But those respondents were exercising their right to react, through verbal means. As I do, to the fury of many who would say they are righteous free speechers.

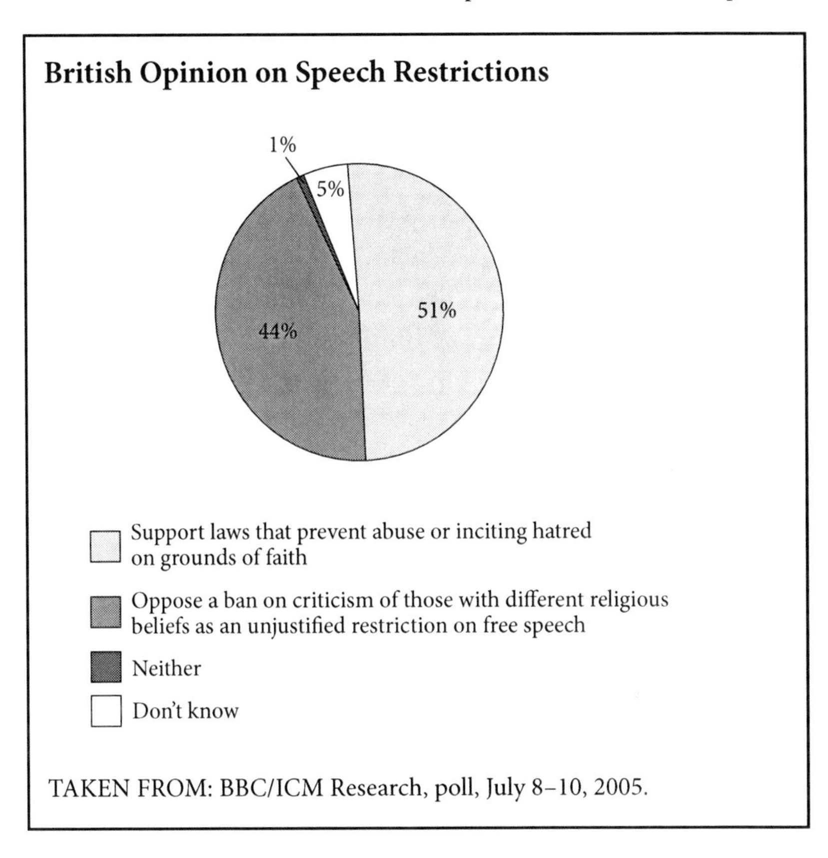

[Scottish comedian] Frankie Boyle will, I expect, feel put upon by Ofcom [Office of Communications, a government-approved communications regulator in the United Kingdom], which lightly slapped his wrist for grotesque TV "jokes" about the disabled son of [British model] Katie Price. The FA [Football Association] is deciding what to do with Wayne Rooney, who swore horridly on TV. The footballer—who has apologised—must be crying into his champagne. I hope he gets his comeuppance. The public space is shared and most people watch what they say to make it less fraught and more livable. We stop ourselves and our kids from saying rude and nasty things because we understand there have to be some social constraints on speech. And if you don't watch your mouth, you have to take what follows.

Limits on Free Speech

In 1919, the US justice Oliver Wendell Holmes decreed that the only limits to freedom of speech were words that activate immediate danger, like a man shouting "Fire!" in a crowded theatre. But what about when individuals set out calculatedly to provoke unrest and anger, which then happens? Like the burning of the Koran. Of course the offended should not rage and die for it—but that was the intention. The inciters are surely as culpable as the man in the theatre. They raise hatred, which eventually leads to violence. Jewish people, Tutsis, Bosnian Muslims, and millions of others were slain easily because words had taken away their humanity. The right-wing press has so demonised asylum seekers that today the UK [United Kingdom] Border Agency presumes all applicants are liars unless they can prove otherwise. Words have institutionalised a grave injustice.

We are not as free as we think, and to argue as if we are is disingenuous.

Young people bullying others through social network sites don't want the victims to try to kill themselves, but many do. It is not immediate, but still evil. Internet abusers never have to pay for the breakages they cause. [Danish philosopher Søren] Kierkegaard worried that newspapers, "a dreadful, disproportionate means of communication," could send "any error into circulation with no thought of responsibility." How much more wanton is new technology? Those protecting the wild web from "regulation" should attend to the severe restrictions on free speech imposed by libel laws, confidentiality agreements, injunctions, and litigious individuals. We are not as free as we think, and to argue as if we are is disingenuous.

Another thing to consider is that most of us are biased. We want some words to be free, and others not. Will the Koran burner be backed by libertarians, atheists and Muslim bashers? Or will he face the same opprobrium as those Muslims who burnt [British Indian writer] Salman Rushdie's book? I await [English writers] Fay Weldon and Ian McEwan's beautifully expressed outrage.

Buddha said: "The wise fashion speech with their thought, sifting it as a grain is sifted through a sieve." We need to be wise to use and preserve our precious freedoms. Sadly, we are not wise.

Viewpoint 3

Canada Clamps Down on Criticism of Israel

Jillian Kestler-D'Amours

In the following viewpoint, the author discusses the anti-Semitic behavior that some claim is on the rise in Canada. Kestler-D'Amours claims that the Canadian Parliamentary Coalition to Combat Antisemitism's (CPCCA's) real purpose seems to be to stifle any pro-Palestine organizing in Canada. She argues that pro-Palestine advocates are labeled as anti-Semitic by the CPCCA because of their inability to participate in other human rights struggles from around the world. Jillian Kestler-D'Amours is a Canadian freelance journalist based in Jerusalem. She regularly contributes to The Electronic Intifada, Inter-Press Service and Free Speech Radio News.

As you read, consider the following questions:

1. According to the author, how many hearings did the CPCCA hold between November 2009 and January 2010?
2. How many recommendations did the CPCCA make in its final report, according to the viewpoint?
3. Who is Thomas Woodley, as stated by the author?

Jillian Kestler-D'Amours, "Canada Clamps Down on Criticism of Israel," Al Jazeera, July 22, 2011. www.aljazeera.com.

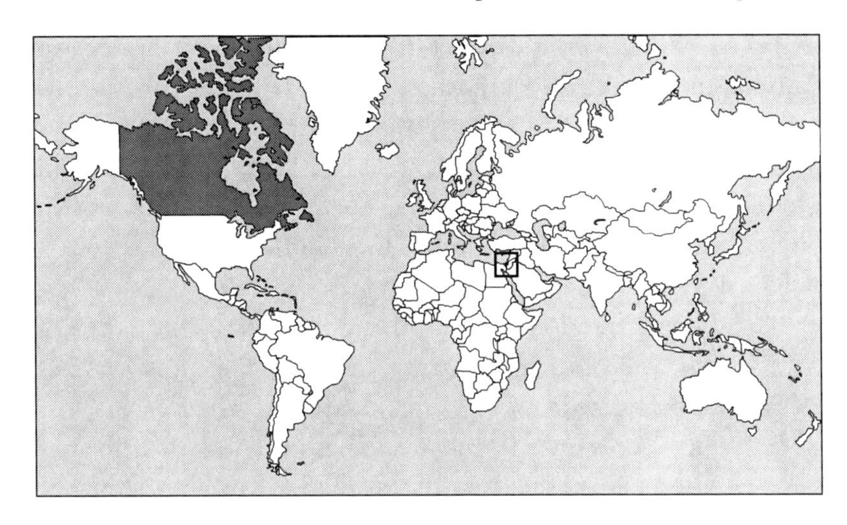

Nearly two years after the first hearings were held in Ottawa, the Canadian Parliamentary Coalition to Combat Antisemitism (CPCCA) released a detailed report on July 7 that found that anti-Semitism is on the rise in Canada, especially on university campuses.

While the CPCCA's final report does contain some cases of real anti-Semitism, the committee has provided little evidence that anti-Semitism has actually increased in Canada in recent years. Instead, it has focused a disproportionate amount of effort and resources on what it calls a so-called "new anti-Semitism": criticism of Israel.

Indeed, the real purpose of the CPCCA coalition seems to be to stifle critiques of Israeli policy and disrupt pro-Palestinian solidarity organizing in Canada, including, most notably, Israeli Apartheid Week events. Many of the CPCCA's findings, therefore, must be rejected as both an attack on freedom of speech and freedom of protest, and as recklessly undermining the fight against real instances of anti-Semitism.

The CPCCA and Its Findings

The Canadian Parliamentary Coalition to Combat Antisemitism (CPCCA) was born out of a conference held in London in February 2009 by the Inter-Parliamentary Committee for Combating Antisemitism. Formed in March 2009 and not directly linked to the Canadian government, or to any NGO or advocacy group, the CPCCA included 22 Canadian Parliament members from across party lines. Former Liberal MP Mario Silva chaired the inquiry panel and Conservative MP Scott Reid led the steering committee.

Between November 2009 and January 2010, the CPCCA held ten separate hearings during which time representatives of various nongovernmental organizations, religious institutions, police departments and Canadian and Israeli universities presented papers meant to assess the level of anti-Semitism in Canada. While groups critical of Israel were denied the chance to address the committee, major Zionist organizations like B'nai Brith Canada, Friends of Simon Wiesenthal Center for Holocaust Studies, and the Canadian Jewish Congress were welcomed.

The CPCCA is supporting a definition whereby individuals who focus their attention on Israeli human rights violations . . . can be labeled as anti-Semitic.

"Much of today's anti-Semitism manifests in anti-Israel agitation around boycotts, divestment and sanctions," said Avi Benlolo, president and CEO of the Friends of Simon Wiesenthal Center for Holocaust Studies, during a hearing in November 2009. "It deploys an unfair double standard against the Jewish state, singling out of Israel alone for one-sided, harsh criticism and calls for punitive actions."

Throughout the consultation process, the CPCCA regularly focused on Canadian university campuses, which were routinely described as hotbeds of anti-Semitism, where Jewish students or students with pro-Israel leanings are often intimidated and threatened. This accusation was made repeatedly, and included in the CPCCA's final report, despite the fact that

Dr. Fred Lowy, president emeritus of Concordia University in Montreal, stated in his address to the CPCCA that, "by and large, Canadian campuses are safe and are not hotbeds of anti-Semitism of any kind".

In its final report, the CPCCA made about two dozen recommendations on how best to fight anti-Semitism in Canada. While the report states that "criticism of Israel is not anti-Semitic, and saying so is wrong", it also found that "singling Israel out for selective condemnation and opprobrium . . . is discriminatory and hateful" and many of its recommendations deal with combating this "new anti-Semitism".

A major recommendation issued by the CPCCA was that the Canadian government should promote the working definition of anti-Semitism used by the European Union Monitoring Centre on Racism and Xenophobia (EUMC). This definition categorizes "applying double standards by requiring of [Israel] a behavior not expected or demanded of any other democratic nation" as anti-Semitic.

In other words, the CPCCA is supporting a definition whereby individuals who focus their attention on Israeli human rights violations, yet don't level an equal amount of condemnation on other states for their human rights violations, can be labeled as anti-Semitic. This is obviously problematic since Palestine solidarity activists—like any other people—have commitments that make it impossible to engage with every issue they are otherwise interested in. They shouldn't be labeled as anti-Semitic due to their inability to participate in every single human rights struggle happening around the world.

Another dangerous recommendation made by the CPCCA was that Canadian university administrators should condemn "discourse, events and speakers which are untrue, harmful, or not in the interest of academic discourse, including Israeli Apartheid Week". Even the use of the word "apartheid" in relation to Israel is anti-Semitic, the CPCCA found, since it amounts to the "denial of the Jewish people their right to self-determination . . . by claiming that the existence of a State of Israel is a racist endeavor".

This clearly violates freedom of speech and an open exchange of ideas at Canadian universities, and also unfairly and inaccurately labels Israeli Apartheid Week (IAW) as anti-Semitic. In reality, IAW has since 2005 brought together respected activists, academics, journalists and cultural figures from around the world, including Judith Butler, Ronnie Kasrils, Noam Chomsky and Ali Abunimah, among others, to openly discuss ideas related to Israel/Palestine.

[Independent Jewish Voices (IJV) Canada opposes] "the CPCCA as an ideologically biased organization with an agenda that will harm free speech and human rights activity in Canada."

IAW provides an educational space for understanding Israel's apartheid policies—as evidenced, for example, through the separate legal systems used by Israelis and Palestinians living in the occupied West Bank or the discriminatory land ownership laws operating inside Israel—and supports the growing campaign for boycott, divestment and sanctions (BDS), which aims to non-violently pressure Israel to respect international law. It is far from the "uniformly well-organized, aggressive [campaign] designed to make the Jewish state and its supporters pariahs" the CPCCA report makes it out to be.

The CPCCA also recommended that the Canadian committee on foreign affairs undertake a study on the United Nations Human Rights Council, "particularly regarding its over-emphasis of alleged human rights abuses by Israel, while ignoring flagrant human rights abuses of other member states".

This clearly demonstrates how the committee has confounded anti-Semitism with criticism of Israel and is prepared to levy dubious suspicions against UN bodies and tarnish Canada's international standing in the process.

In a statement released on July 8, Thomas Woodley, president of Canadians for Justice and Peace in the Middle East (CJPME), said that the CPCCA's recommendations, "if implemented, will inhibit public discussion of Israel's conduct".

"CJPME believes that conclusions and recommendations generated by a process in which the same body—the CPCCA—is prosecutor, jury, and judge, are not credible. Although a few of the witnesses recounted incidents that were indeed indicative of genuine anti-Semitism, many were complaining about merely being exposed to criticism of Israel's conduct," the CJPME press release stated.

Independent Jewish Voices (IJV) Canada also criticized the committee, stating that "the CPCCA's goal is to criminalize criticism of Israel and Zionism, not to hold impartial hearings. Therefore, we oppose the CPCCA as an ideologically biased organization with an agenda that will harm free speech and human rights activity in Canada. We oppose the CPCCA's Orwellian distortion of anti-Semitism. It is a danger to both Canadian liberties and to the genuine and necessary fight against anti-Semitism."

Reflection of Official Canadian Policy

While labeling critics of Israeli policy as anti-Semitic is nothing new, the level at which this accusation is now being used in Canadian discourse must be seen as a reflection of the Canadian government's official and current policy on the Middle East.

"When Israel, the only country in the world whose very existence is under attack, is consistently and conspicuously singled out for condemnation, I believe we are morally obligated to take a stand. Demonization, double standards, delegitimization, the three D's, it is the responsibility of us all to stand up to them," Canadian prime minister Stephen Harper said in 2010 at the Ottawa Conference on Combating Antisemitism, which was supported by the CPCCA. Harper added:

"Harnessing disparate anti-American, anti-Semitic and anti-Western ideologies, it targets the Jewish people by targeting the Jewish homeland, Israel, as the source of injustice and conflict in the world and uses, perversely, the language of human rights to do so. We must be relentless in exposing this new anti-Semitism for what it is."

Under Harper, Canada has routinely defended Israeli intransigence and disregard for international law and the human rights of the Palestinian people under its control. In return, trade cooperation and military and security technologies ties have been strengthened between the two states.

In May of this year, it was reported that Harper was adamantly opposed to making any reference to the 1967 borders in a G8 summit statement calling for renewed Israeli-Palestinian negotiations. Far-right Israeli foreign minister Avigdor Lieberman thanked Harper for his position, and stated, "Canada is a true friend of Israel".

In 2010, Canada announced it would discontinue its financial contributions to the United Nations Relief and Works Agency (UNRWA), the organization that provides support and resources to approximately 4.7m registered Palestinian refugees in Jordan, Lebanon, Syria and the occupied Palestinian territories, and funnels the money into greater policing and security institutions run by the unelected and corrupt Palestinian Authority leadership instead.

In January 2009, as the Israeli army continued its disproportionate attack on the besieged civilian population in Gaza that left 1,400 Palestinians dead in the span of three weeks, Canada was the only country out of 47 that voted against a motion at the United Nations Human Rights Council condemning the Israeli violence. In addition to providing diplomatic cover for Israel, the Canadian government has attacked and cut funding to various nongovernmental organizations working on issues related to Israel/Palestine, including Kairos churches and Alternatives International.

Canadian minister of citizenship, immigration and multiculturalism Jason Kenney, who led the formation of the Canadian Parliamentary Coalition to Combat Antisemitism (CPCCA) and is an ex officio member, has also repeatedly alleged that the Canadian Arab Federation promotes anti-Semitism and hatred. While Kenney never backed up these claims, the Canadian Arab Federation's contracts with the government—which helped finance language programs for Toronto-area immigrants (the majority of whom are of Chinese origin)—were not renewed in 2009.

This is something that Canadians, and people everywhere, should be adamantly against.

Undermining the Fight Against Real Anti-Semitism

Anti-Semitism, like all other forms of racism, is appalling and must be strongly and unequivocally condemned. But by defining legitimate criticism of Israeli policy and pro-Palestinian activism in Canada as anti-Semitic, the CPCCA is not only threatening free speech and freedom of protest, but it is also undermining the fight against real cases of anti-Semitism and weakening the seriousness with which such cases should be dealt.

This is something that Canadians, and people everywhere, should be adamantly against.

VIEWPOINT 4

Canada Is Correct to Recognize That Free Speech Should Not Include Anti-Semitism

Avi Benlolo

In the following viewpoint, Avi Benlolo argues that Canada was right to sign the Ottawa Protocol on Combating Antisemitism, which declares that anti-Semitism will not be tolerated. Benlolo argues that anti-Semitism is a problem in Canada, particularly on university campuses, where he warns that free speech is not justified when used to spread hatred toward Jewish students. Benlolo is a Canadian human rights activist as well as president and chief executive officer of the Friends of Simon Wiesenthal Center for Holocaust Studies (FSWC).

As you read, consider the following questions:

1. The author claims that by signing the Ottawa protocol Canada recognized anti-Semitism as what?
2. How many countries declared that they would not take part in Durban III, a United Nations (UN) conference, according to Benlolo?

Avi Benlolo, "Canada Gets Tough on Anti-Semitism," *Huffington Post Canada*, September 21, 2011.

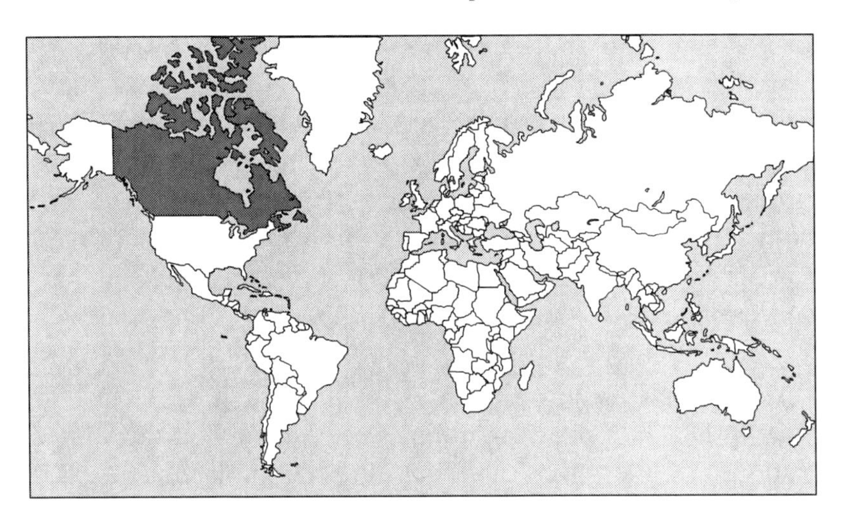

3. Benlolo calls for college universities in Canada to end what event?

The government of Canada took a historic step yesterday [September 20, 2011] by signing the Ottawa Protocol [on Combating Antisemitism]. By doing so, it recognized anti-Semitism as a pernicious evil and a global threat against the Jewish people, the State of Israel and free, democratic countries everywhere. As Prime Minister Stephen Harper has noted, "Those who would hate and destroy the Jewish people would ultimately hate and destroy the rest of us as well."

The Ottawa Protocol Against Anti-Semitism

The protocol is a declaration that hatred of this nature will not be tolerated in this country. It sets out an action plan for supporting initiatives that combat anti-Semitism and provides a framework for other nations to follow.

It also sets out a vibrant definition of anti-Semitism which, for the first time in history, links anti-Semitism to the denial of the right Jewish people have to their ancestral homeland—the State of Israel. This, in fact, is what sets post–World War

II anti-Semitism apart from its historic roots. Today's anti-Semitism is all about denial: denial of the legitimacy of Zionism as a Jewish movement to reclaim the land of Israel; denial of a Jewish history in connection to the holy land and, in particular, the centrality of Jerusalem to the Jewish people; denial of the Holocaust (while at the same time accusing Jews of Nazism); and denial of Jews to live free of anti-Semitism, hate and intolerance.

In announcing the protocol, Foreign Minister John Baird has expressed his government's unequivocal support for the State of Israel. In referring to this week's turmoil at the United Nations [UN] and the Palestinian threat to unilaterally declare a state, Baird said, "Canada will not stand behind Israel at the United Nations, we will stand right beside it. It is never a bad thing to do the right thing."

Today's anti-Semitism is all about denial.

According to Baird, more and more countries are refusing to participate in the UN conference dubbed "Durban III"—otherwise known as an anti-Semitic hate fest which began as a human rights forum in South Africa in 2001; the forum ultimately degenerated into an anti-Semitic slinging match in which repressive Arab and African countries blamed all the problems facing their own countries and the world on Israel. The governments of France, New Zealand and Poland (today) joined Canada and 10 other Western nations this week by declaring they will not take part.

Anti-Semitism in Canada

Unquestionably, the government of Canada's stance on Israel is based on the principle of standing by your friends—especially when they are democracies and advocates for human rights. Most Jewish leaders would agree that Israel is indeed Canada's greatest ally in the fight against hate and intolerance.

Examples of Anti-Semitism

Examples of the ways in which anti-Semitism manifests itself with regard to the State of Israel taking into account the overall context could include:

- Denying the Jewish people their right to self-determination, e.g., by claiming that the existence of a State of Israel is a racist endeavour.
- Applying double standards by requiring of it behaviour not expected or demanded of any other democratic nation.
- Using the symbols and images associated with classic anti-Semitism (e.g., claims of Jews killing Jesus or blood libel) to characterize Israel or Israelis.
- Drawing comparisons of contemporary Israeli policy to that of the Nazis.
- Holding Jews collectively responsible for actions of the State of Israel.

However, criticism of Israel similar to that levelled against any other country cannot be regarded as anti-Semitic.

Let it be clear: Criticism of Israel is not anti-Semitic, and saying so is wrong. But singling Israel out for selective condemnation and opprobrium—let alone denying its right to exist or seeking its destruction—is discriminatory and hateful, and not saying so is dishonest.

Inter-Parliamentary Coalition for Combating Antisemitism (ICCA), "Ottawa Protocol on Combating Antisemitism," Canadian Parliamentary Coalition to Combat Antisemitism, 2010.

But the fight against hatred and anti-Semitism must be won here in Canada as well. The Ottawa protocol is mostly the result of a report published this summer by a Canadian Parliamentary Coalition to Combat Antisemitism which was comprised of leading Canadian politicians who volunteered their time to probe the increasing and alarming tide of anti-Semitism in Canada.

In a letter accompanying the report, chairs of the inquiry panel and the steering committee Mario Silva and Scott Reid wrote, "The inquiry panel's conclusion, unfortunately, is that the scourge of anti-Semitism is a growing threat in Canada, especially on the campuses of our universities." The report cites numerous examples of anti-Semitism on various campuses including the infamous incident in 2009 when Jewish students at York University were chased and barricaded themselves in the Hillel lounge while a mob outside taunted them with anti-Semitic slurs. The list of examples is quite long and disturbing.

[Universities] should state unequivocally that freedom of speech should not be abused to provide a cover for anti-Semitism.

Anti-Semitism on University Campuses

Universities should take note of the report and the signing of the Ottawa protocol. They should put an immediate end to hateful and fallacious events like Israeli Apartheid Week; they should state unequivocally that freedom of speech should not be abused to provide a cover for anti-Semitism; they should ensure that Jewish students feel welcome on campus and that their learning environment should be freed from anti-Israel occurrences and finally, universities must become accountable for allowing their private property to be venues for hateful conduct among students.

The Ottawa Protocol [on Combating] Antisemitism is a template for every Canadian to consider. But it is especially a document of significance for universities that have allowed themselves to become vehicles of hatred and complicit in its promotion. As my friend, Professor Irwin Cotler said last night at the Ottawa [protocol] signing ceremony, anti-Semitism is not only the longest known form of hatred in the history of humanity—it is the only form of hatred that is truly global.

Every person of conscience should take note of the Ottawa protocol and never forget the lessons of the Holocaust when the world was silent.

Viewpoint 5

India's Restrictions on Free Speech Contradict Its Constitution

Karan Singh Tyagi

In the following viewpoint, Karan Singh Tyagi argues that both traditional rationales and the Indian Constitution support freedom of speech. He contends that the recent banning of a film in the Indian state of Tamil Nadu is misguided as it is based only on the possibility of social disruption rather than on any overt call to violence. In opposition to such a ban, Tyagi points to three traditional rationales for freedom of speech that he claims are reflected in the Indian Constitution. Tyagi is an associate attorney with an international law firm in Paris and a graduate of Harvard University Law School.

As you read, consider the following questions:

1. Tyagi draws an analogy between the banning of *Dam 999* by the Indian state of Tamil Nadu and what action of Dionysius?
2. According to the author, the self-government rationale for free speech was first enunciated in what US Supreme Court case?

Karan Singh Tyagi, "Free Speech and Indian Dionysius," *The Hindu* (India), December 2, 2011.

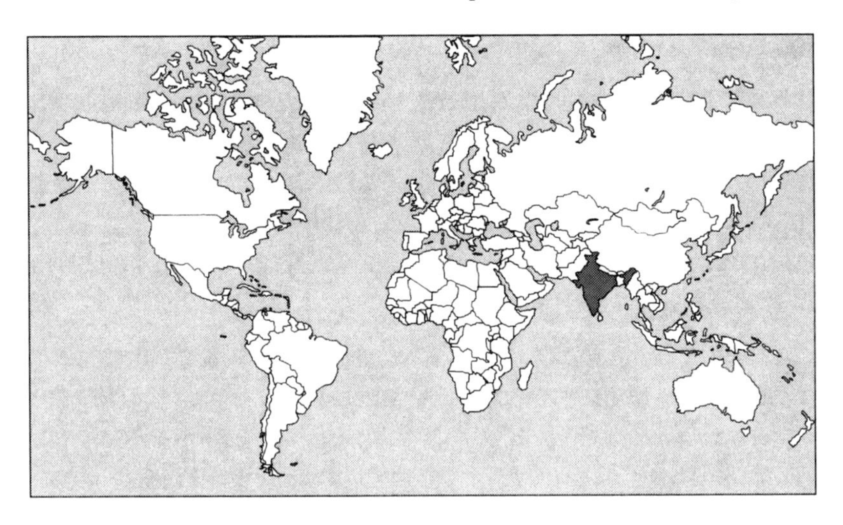

3. What two foundational strands does Tyagi claim are in the Indian Constitution, drawing on the work of Granville Austin?

Though the Indian Constitution reflects the classical rationales of free speech, the state has time and again punished thought and suppressed ideas.

[Greek biographer] Plutarch's *Life of Dion* contains an interesting anecdote of [Greek leader] Dionysius, an avowed and established tyrant, killing his captain, Marsyas. Marsyas had dreamt of cutting Dionysius's throat, and Dionysius killed Marsyas on account of his dream. He based his decision on the assumption that Marsyas would not have dreamt of such a thing by night if he had not thought of it by day.

In his seminal work *The Spirit of the Laws*, [French philosopher] Montesquieu picks up this story to reason that Dionysius's was a most tyrannical action; for, though cutting Dionysius's throat had been the subject of Marsyas's thoughts, he had made no attempt towards it. "*The laws do not take upon them to punish any other than overt acts. The thought must be joined with some sort of action*", concluded Montesquieu.

Banned Speech in India

It can safely be said that Montesquieu's words are completely lost on the Indian state, and it has time and again assumed the character of a present-day Dionysius by punishing mere thoughts. The latest Dionysius is the Tamil Nadu state government, which has banned the screening of the movie *Dam 999* in the state.

Dam 999 is apparently a love story set against the backdrop of the Mullaperiyar dam controversy. The Tamil Nadu government has banned the screening of the movie on the ground that it might lead to *public order* problems in the state. This amounts to suppression of ideas that supposedly pose a threat to public order.

It must be emphasised that there is a difference between goading people to resort to violence and expressing a view on the dam controversy. The former is an overt act the government can rightfully prohibit. The latter is the communication of an idea, which the government must not proscribe. The common view in India is that any communication having a tendency to lead to violence can be suppressed. This in turn enables the government to suppress any idea.

Indeed, the history of independent India is replete with examples of the government curbing free speech: We were the first country to ban Salman Rushdie's book *The Satanic Verses*; Rohinton Mistry's *Such a Long Journey* was dropped by the Mumbai University from its syllabus; Delhi University did the same with A.K. Ramanujan's essay "Three Hundred Ramayanas"; makers of the movie *Rockstar* were forced to blur the Tibetan flag in the "Sadda Haq" song; and movies like *Desh-Drohi, Bandit Queen, The Da Vinci Code, Fire* and many others have been banned by state governments. These examples are just the tip of the iceberg, and there are numerous other instances where the government has chilled speech in the country.

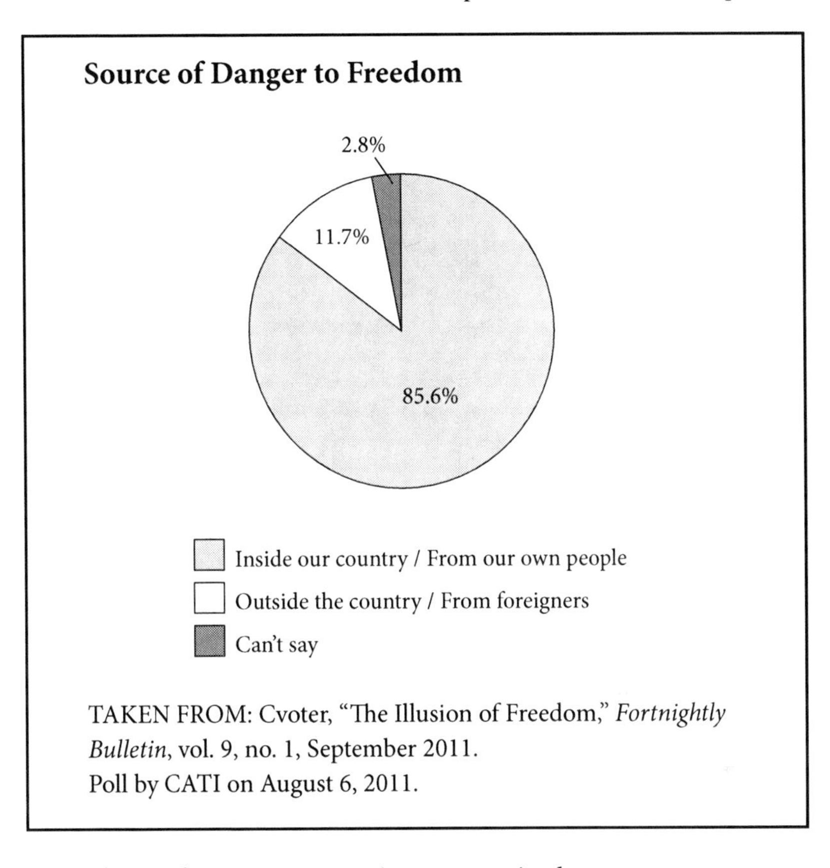

TAKEN FROM: Cvoter, "The Illusion of Freedom," *Fortnightly Bulletin*, vol. 9, no. 1, September 2011.
Poll by CATI on August 6, 2011.

Why is this so? One major reason is that governments act without an understanding of the underlying rationale of free speech. They act without knowing why a country like India needs to grant effective protection to freedom of speech.

The common view in India is that any communication having a tendency to lead to violence can be suppressed. This in turn enables the government to suppress any idea.

The Rationales for Freedom of Speech

Broadly speaking, there are three main rationales for protection of freedom of speech, which are also reflected in the vision with which our Constitution was drafted.

The first is the *self-government* rationale, which provides that it is indispensable to protect free speech for a robust democratic process. Protection of free speech is essential for people to communicate on political matters, which in turn enables them to fully participate in democratic affairs. This rationale, though identified with the work of [English philosopher] Alexander Meiklejohn, was first enunciated by Justice [Louis] Brandeis of the U.S. Supreme Court in *Whitney v. California* [(1927)].

The second rationale is fashioned on *laissez-faire* in the economic realm and conceives that, in a *marketplace of ideas*, the better ideas eventually prevail through competition. Under this *marketplace of ideas* rationale, all kinds of speech are permitted on the understanding that ruinous speech will fail the market assessment test and will eventually be discarded. This justification for free speech is that it is essential in a society's *search for truth*, which will ultimately emerge after a competition of all ideas in the marketplace. In the words of Justice [Oliver Wendell] Holmes of the U.S. Supreme Court, "*the best test of truth is the power of the thought to get itself accepted in the competition of the market*" [*Abrams v. United States* (1919)].

The last rationale treats freedom of speech as promotion of every individual's *self-fulfillment and autonomy*. This rationale posits that protection of free speech is essential for human identity. To be fully human, it is essential to protect thoughts.

The Indian Constitution

Fascinatingly, the classical rationales for free speech are also reflected in the theoretical underpinnings of the Indian Constitution. [Historian] Granville Austin, in his exposition on the Indian Constitution (*Working a Democratic Constitution: The Indian Experience*), indicates that the core vision of the Indian Constitution can be summed up as having the following foundational strands: (i) protecting national unity and establishing the institutions and spirit of democracy; and (ii) fostering a social revolution to better the lot of Indians.

The spirit of democracy can be strengthened if citizens are able to fully participate in democratic affairs (*self-government rationale*). Similarly, for fostering a social revolution and to improve the lot of Indians, it is necessary that the society engages itself in the *pursuit of truth*, and all citizens be given every opportunity to realise their potential (*self-fulfillment and autonomy*). These rationales for free speech thus represent an important resource in our constitutional tradition—a resource that the Indian state keeps ignoring at its own peril.

The classical rationales for free speech are also reflected in the theoretical underpinnings of the Indian Constitution.

Thus, if India has to evolve, a better understanding of our constitutional traditions is a must. And if anti-speech acts persist, it reflects nothing but the Dionysius nature of the Indian state.

Periodical and Internet Sources Bibliography

The following articles have been selected to supplement the diverse views presented in this chapter.

Abeer Allam	"Online Law Curbs Saudi Freedom of Expression," *Financial Times*, April 6, 2011.
Amnesty International	"Israel Anti-Boycott Law an Attack on Freedom of Expression," July 12, 2011. www.amnesty.org.
Australian	"Assault on Free Speech Should Be Offensive to All," September 29, 2011.
John Bussey	"Facebook's Test in China: What Price Free Speech?," *Wall Street Journal*, June 10, 2011.
Sadanand Dhume	"Blows to India's Free Speech," *National* (Abu Dhabi, UAE), February 6, 2010.
Jacob G. Hornberger	"Freedom of Speech in China and America," Future of Freedom Foundation, August 21, 2008. www.fff.org.
Jacob Mchangama	"The OIC vs. Freedom of Expression: Their Change of Tactics Imperils Speech Worldwide," *National Review Online*, April 7, 2011. www.nationalreview.com.
Jo-Ann Mort	"Remember Havel, and Don't Forget Hungary," *Dissent*, December 22, 2011.
Brian Palmer	"Is There Freedom of Speech in China? Only Symbolically," *Slate*, October 8, 2010. www.slate.com.
Paula Schriefer	"The New Threat to Freedom of Expression," *Christian Science Monitor*, March 30, 2009.
David Waddington	"Free Speech Is Not Hateful," *Guardian* (UK), October 6, 2009.

Chapter 2

Media Freedom and Freedom of the Press

VIEWPOINT 1

Assaults on Writers Throughout the World Have Increased in Recent Years

Marian Botsford Fraser

In the following viewpoint, Marian Botsford Fraser argues that the scale of assaults against writers worldwide has increased recently. Fraser contends that writers, journalists, and bloggers all over the world are imprisoned, tortured, and murdered for farcical reasons. She claims that the violations on freedom of expression occur even in light of international human rights covenants, and she contends that it is important that writers suffering such abuses not be forgotten. Fraser is a Canadian writer.

As you read, consider the following questions:

1. What Chinese Nobel Peace Prize recipient received an eleven-year prison sentence, according to Fraser?
2. What Vietnamese poet spent almost twenty-seven years in prison for his poems, according to the author?
3. According to Fraser, what Nigerian activist was hanged in 1995?

"We must stop the practice of viewing words as crimes." Those measured words are from Charter 08, the call for democracy by Chinese writers, dissidents and citizens that

Marian Botsford Fraser, "Fighting the Global Assault on Freedom of Expression," *The Guardian* (UK), November 15, 2010.

has earned the poet and scholar Liu Xiaobo an 11-year prison sentence and the 2010 Nobel Peace Prize.

The Writers in Prison Committee

It doesn't take very many words to set off a reaction that ends badly for writers. Liu Xiaobo's imprisonment is for seven published phrases deemed "subversive"; these sentences consist of just 224 Chinese characters. Writers have been sentenced in the past year [November 15, 2009 to November 15, 2010] for hooliganism (Azerbaijan) and defacing a street sign (Georgia). They have been jailed for writing about the environment in Panama and Morocco; handed a three-year sentence for songwriting (Cameroon); a five-year sentence for blogging (Tibet); a 19-year sentence for blogging (Iran). Abducted in Yemen, beaten in Sudan, detained in Mauritania and killed by the dozen in Mexico.

For 50 years the Writers in Prison Committee [WiPC] of PEN International has monitored the practice of viewing words as crimes and treating writers as criminals. PEN International, founded in 1921, is arguably the oldest freedom of expression organisation in the world. Until 1960, PEN's advocacy took the form of impassioned pleas on behalf of individual writers such as Arthur Koestler and Federico García Lorca in the 1930s, and Boris Pasternak in the 1950s.

The PEN charter, binding its members to the protection of freedom of expression and resistance to censorship, was an intellectual precursor of article 19 of the Universal Declaration of Human Rights. Concerns for colleagues imprisoned, executed, tortured through times of war, peace, revolution, and détente generated speeches at congresses, letters of support, telegrams to offending governments and an embrace of exiled writers. But in 1960 this tradition of solidarity and compassion became, formally, a committee.

On 24 July 1960, at a congress in Rio [de Janeiro, Brazil], PEN's general secretary, David Carver, produced a list of 56 imprisoned writers created by a three-person committee—seven writers imprisoned in Albania, 25 in Czechoslovakia, 13 in Hungary, two in France and nine in Romania. That committee of three is now a committee of more than 70 PEN centres worldwide, and the WiPC casebook now often contains the names of more than 900 writers, journalists, publishers, editors and bloggers.

It doesn't take very many words to set off a reaction that ends badly for writers.

The Attacks on Writers

What does not change is the often farcical nature of the sentence: Albanian poet Musine Kokalari was serving a 20-year sentence for being an "enemy of the people" when the WiPC was formed in 1960. Vietnamese poet Nguyen Chi Thien spent almost 27 years in prison for his "politically irreverent poems"; Egyptian writer and physician Nawal El Saadawi wrote *Memoirs from the Women's Prison* during her incarceration for "crimes against the state"; in 2008, young student Parwez Kambakhsh was sentenced to death in Afghanistan for blasphemy (by downloading material about the prophet Muhammad).

In some cases, the judgment is death: In 1995 Ogoni environmental activist writer Ken Saro-Wiwa was hanged in Nigeria despite an unprecedented international outcry over his summary murder trial. The murders of Russian journalist Anna Politkovskaya and Turkish editor Hrant Dink remain unresolved.

What has changed is the scale of assault on freedom of expression. This past year, we've seen mass killings of citizens including writers in Mexico and the Philippines, and mass arrests of writers, journalists, bloggers in Iran; more than 40 writers are imprisoned in China and almost 40 in Iran.

In Mexico, more than 30 journalists have been murdered or disappeared since 2006, at least nine so far this year. Since November 2009 almost 40 writers have been killed or disappeared worldwide. More than 200 writers are serving very long sentences, in extremely poor health in remote prisons in China, Vietnam and Burma.

And where individual writers were once targeted in papal edicts and book burnings, the focus in a highly literate, interconnected world is now on the suppression of people's right to read and on the abuse of due process. Communications devices and media are shut down within borders and beyond (China, Iran, Burma [also known as Myanmar], Vietnam, Tunisia, Uzbekistan). Because of an unnerving climate of impunity (notably in Mexico, Eritrea, Somalia), a shroud of silence smothers inquiry, investigation, publication, and the engagement of citizens.

Many countries signatory to international human rights covenants flagrantly abuse the rights of their citizens.

Making Imprisoned Writers Known

PEN gives a name and a face to the issue of censorship. People without names can be executed or "disappear" with impunity. Many countries signatory to international human rights covenants flagrantly abuse the rights of their citizens. Who are the men and women whose rights are being violated? Who is in prison, or executed, or driven into exile?

The individual writer is both a person, on whose behalf we ask for mercy and justice, and also a symbol. The terrible irony in Ken Saro-Wiwa's case is that, precisely at the moment his name was uttered during a 1995 meeting of the British Commonwealth—the public arena most significant to the Nigerian regime—he was hanged by that same government. It was the opposite of how magic works in fairy tales like

Writers Killed, January to October, 2011

Location	Name	Occupation
Bahrain	Karim Fakhrawi	Journalist
Bolivia	David Nino De Guzman	Journalist
Brazil	Valério Nascimento	Journalist
Brazil	Ednaldo Figueira	Blogger
Brazil	Auro Ida	Columnist
China	Sun Hongjie	Reporter
Colombia	Luis Eduardo Gomez	Journalist
India	Umesh Rajput	Reporter
India	Jyotirmoy Dey	Editor
India	Ramesh Singla	Journalist
Iraq	Hila Al Ahmad	Journalist
Ivory Coast	Lago Sylvain	Journalist
Mexico	Susana Chavez	Poet
Mexico	Noel Lopez Olguin	Journalist
Mexico	Pablo Ruelas Barraza	Journalist
Mexico	Miguel Angel Lopez Velasco	Journalist
Mexico	Angel Castillo Corona	Journalist
Mexico	Yolanda Ordaz De La Cruz	Reporter
Mexico	Humberto Millan Salazar	Columnist
Mexico	Ana María Yarce Viveros	Reporter
Mexico	María Elizabeth Marcias Castro	Blogger
Pakistan	Ilyas Nazar	Journalist
Pakistan	Zaman Ibrahim	Reporter
Pakistan	Syed Saleem Shahzad	Journalist
Pakistan	Muneer Sharik	Journalist
Palestine Authority	Vittorio Arrigoni	Journalist
Philippines	Jonson Pascual	Journalist
Russia/North Ossetia	Shamil Dzhikayev	Poet
Syria	Ibrahim Qashoush	Poet
Venezuela	Wilfred Iván Ojeda Peralta	Columnist
Yemen	Mohamed Yahia Al-Malayia	Journalist

TAKEN FROM: Pen International, November 15, 2011. www.pen-international.org.

Rumpelstiltskin. But, arguably, the fact that writers such as Aung San Suu Kyi and Liu Xiaobo and Parwez Kambakhsh became well known is one reason they are still alive.

Curiously, book burning is back in vogue. In September 2010, a Christian fundamentalist preacher in Florida threatened to burn hundreds of copies of the Qur'an. In Mumbai last month, copies of Rohinton Mistry's 20-year-old novel *Such a Long Journey* were burned. Book burning and the banning of blogs spring from the same impulse: fear of the word.

I'm often asked: "Does PEN's work have any impact?" The Syrian poet Faraj Bayrakdar spent 13 years in prison for the crime of belonging to an illegal political organisation. He wrote recently: "During the first 10 years of my detention I felt I was part of that same tragedy by which many throughout history have been oppressed by blind forces from which there is no escape. [But] later when news leaked through about what PEN International [and other organisations] were doing for me . . . I realised that I had not been forgotten. For prisoners, the thought that they are forgotten is a sort of spiritual death."

VIEWPOINT 2

Media Censorship in China

Isabella Bennett

In the following viewpoint, Isabella Bennett argues that although China's constitution gives its citizens freedoms of speech and the press, in reality press freedom is hampered. Bennett contends that censorship in China takes place through a variety of channels, and many journalists have been punished under vague guidelines. She claims that largely because of the Internet, many Chinese are subverting the media controls and pushing for more freedom. Bennett is a research associate for the Council on Foreign Relations.

As you read, consider the following questions:

1. According to Bennett, China amended its Law on Guarding State Secrets in 2010 in what way?
2. What three Chinese agencies does the author identify as monitoring media content?
3. Bennett cites the US State Department as estimating that China has approximately how many Internet monitors?

Introduction

The Chinese government has long tried to keep a tight rein on traditional and new media to prevent any challenges to its political authority. This has often entailed, watchdog groups

Isabella Bennett, "Media Censorship in China," Council on Foreign Relations, March 7, 2011.

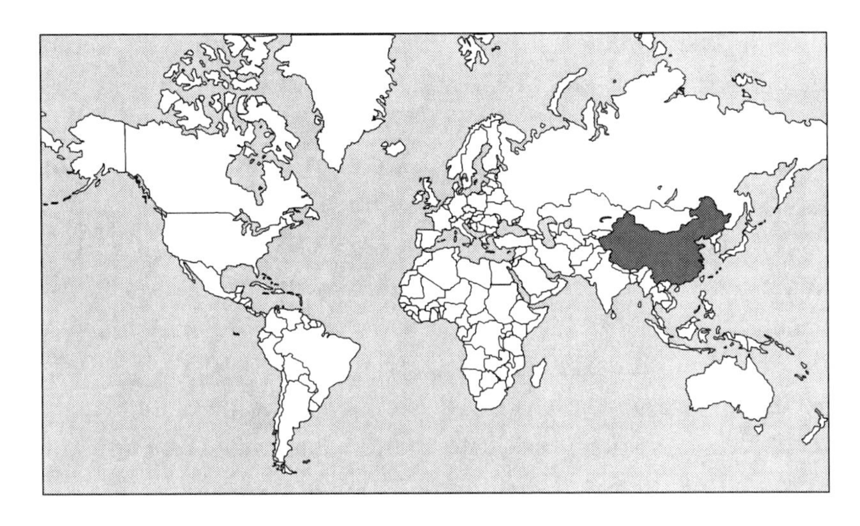

say, strict media controls using monitoring systems, shutting down publications or websites, and jailing of dissident journalists and blogger/activists. China's censorship of its media again grabbed headlines in early 2011, when, following an online appeal for Chinese citizens to emulate the revolutions in the Middle East, the government clamped down on foreign media, arrested dissidents, and mobilized thousands of policemen. Google's battle with the Chinese government over Internet censorship in China and the awarding of the 2010 Nobel Peace Prize to jailed Chinese activist Liu Xiaobo have also drawn increased international attention to media censorship in China. At the same time, the country's burgeoning economy has allowed for greater diversity in China's media coverage, and experts say the growing Chinese demand for information is testing the regime's control over the media.

What Is the Official Media Policy in China?

As China becomes a major player in the global economy, authorities in Beijing are trying to balance the need for more information with their goal of controlling content and maintaining power. CFR senior fellow Elizabeth C. Economy says the Chinese government is in a state of "schizophrenia" about media policy as it "goes back and forth, testing the line, knowing they need press freedom—and the information it provides—but worried about opening the door to the type of freedoms that could lead to the regime's downfall."

China's constitution affords its citizens freedoms of speech and press, but Chinese law includes media regulations with vague language that authorities use to claim stories endanger the country by sharing state secrets. In April 2010, the Chinese government revised its existing Law on Guarding State Secrets to tighten its control over information flows. The amendment extended requirements to Internet companies and telecommunications operators to cooperate with Chinese authorities in investigations into leaks of state secrets. But as many observers note, the definition of state secrets in China remains vague and thus could be used to censor any information the authorities deem as harmful to their political or economic interests. "In the new law, the definition of state secrets remains as sweeping as the original law and still fails to comply with international human rights standards," says the nongovernmental advocacy group Human Rights in China.

As China becomes a major player in the global economy, authorities in Beijing are trying to balance the need for more information with their goal of controlling content and maintaining power.

In May 2010, the government issued its first white paper on the Internet in which it emphasized the concept of "Internet sovereignty," requiring all Internet users in China, including foreign organizations and individuals, to abide by Chinese laws and regulations. Analyst Rebecca MacKinnon, an expert on global Internet policy, writes "the regime actually uses the Internet not only to extend its control but also to enhance its legitimacy."

How Free Is Chinese Media?

The watchdog group Reporters Without Borders ranked China 171 out of 178 countries in its 2010 worldwide index of press freedom. Journalists face harassment and prison terms for violating rules laid down by the government and are therefore pressured into "self-censorship." CFR press fellow Matt Pottinger explains that Chinese media disseminators usually employ their own monitors to ensure political acceptability of their content.

Censorship guidelines are often circulated weekly from the Communist Party propaganda department and the government Bureau of Internet Affairs to prominent editors. A leaked March 2010 version offers some insight into the prohibitions listed.

China's media is undergoing a process of commercialization, which some observers believe is leading to growing competition, diversified content, and an increase in investigative reporting by Chinese news agencies. Only state agencies can own media in China, but there is creeping privatization. China News Network Corporation (CNC), a twenty-four-hour global news network launched in July 2010, for example, is reportedly half privately financed.

According to a government report, the number of publications has soared in recent years, with over eight thousand magazines, more than two thousand newspapers, and some 374 television stations in the country. However, Pottinger argues that the plethora of newspapers has not delivered plurality to the media landscape in China. The myriad new publications remain "a populist, socialist media, just as controlled by the government," he says. "The seemingly chatty, freewheeling press is not really freewheeling at all. The Chinese Communist Party is just more cunning about how it controls public opinion."

Certain websites that the government deems potentially dangerous are blocked during periods of controversy such as the BBC's Chinese language website, the *New York Times*' website, and Wikipedia. Specific material deemed a threat to political stability such as controversial photos, search terms, or particular iPhone applications are also banned.

What Are the Primary Censoring Agencies in China?

More than a dozen government bodies are involved in reviewing and enforcing laws related to information flow within, into, and from China. The most powerful monitoring body is the Communist Party's Central Propaganda Department (CPD), which coordinates with General Administration of Press and Publication (GAPP) and State Administration of Radio, Film and Television (SARFT) to make sure content promotes party doctrine. Xinhua, the state news agency, is considered a propaganda tool by press freedom organizations. The CPD gives media outlets directives restricting coverage of politically sensitive topics—such as protests, Tibet, and Taiwan.

More than a dozen government bodies are involved in reviewing and enforcing laws related to information flow within, into, and from China.

The CPD guidelines are enforced through directives issued to heads of media outlets, demanding that they kill controversial stories and instructing how to cover delicate topics. For example, in March 2010, thirteen daily Chinese newspapers were censored and threatened with punishment when they published a joint editorial calling for the elimination of "hukou," a household registration system that limits the access of rural migrant workers to public services guaranteed to urban residents. The editorial was removed from the newspapers' websites within hours of its posting.

Journalists who do not follow the rules face reprisals in the workplace or, worse, prison terms. Tan Zuoren was sentenced to five years in prison for drawing attention to government corruption and poor construction of school buildings that collapsed and killed thousands of children during the 2008 earthquake in Sichuan province. All inquiries into the issue were blocked by the Chinese government and Zuoren's volunteers were also harassed or beaten.

Publicizing the CPD guidelines also invites punishment, as they may be classified as "state secrets," such as in the case of Shi Tao, a journalist detained in 2004 who is serving a ten-year sentence for posting an online summary describing the CPD's instructions for how to report the fifteen-year anniversary of events at Tiananmen Square.

Pottinger adds that on top of such national restrictions, provincial and local officials release their own directives. Oftentimes, these directives can be detrimental to public health, as in 2008 when local government officials delayed reports of contaminated milk that sickened hundreds of thousands of children.

How Does China Exert Media Controls?

The Chinese government employs a diverse range of methods to induce journalists to censor themselves rather than risk punishment. Tactics include dismissals and demotions; authorities also sue journalists for libel, impose fines or close news outlets. Furthermore, it is not uncommon for journalists who overstep boundaries to be imprisoned. As of December 2010, China was tied with Iran for the most jailed journalists in a single country with at least thirty-four journalists imprisoned according to the Committee to Protect Journalists.

Reporters Without Borders estimates that seventy-seven "netizens" and cyber dissidents are also jailed. Chinese rights activist Liu Xiaobo was sentenced to eleven years in prison for publishing controversial opinions on the Internet and calling

"Chinese Screen Saver," cartoon by Signe Wilkinson's Editorial Cartoons, Cartoonist Group. Copyright © by Signe Wilkinson. All rights reserved. Reproduced by permission.

for democratic reforms and freedom of speech in Charter 08, which earned him the Nobel Peace Prize. Censors reacted fiercely to block the news about the Nobel from penetrating China. Beijing refused to release Liu from prison for the Nobel ceremony and stepped up anti-Nobel rhetoric to discredit the award.

How Does China Control the Influence of Foreign Media?

China requires foreign correspondents to get permission before making reporting trips within the country, and reporters often face harassment if they cover delicate issues. All inbound data from foreign Internet sources is filtered through one of three computer centers in Beijing, Shanghai, and Guangzhou where key words alert authorities of provocative content.

As part of its bid to host the 2008 Olympics, China promised to relax constraints, but critics accuse China of reneging on its promise. The Foreign Correspondents' Club of China reported 178 cases of interference (including detention, harassment, property destruction, and violence) with foreign media in 2008. Some journalists and bloggers arrested before and after the 2008 Beijing Olympics remain in prison as of February 2011. In addition, China continues to filter foreign (and domestic) content on the Internet—in many cases using technology provided by U.S. companies as this Backgrounder notes.

In response to the early 2011 protests that rocked the Middle East and led to the ouster of prominent autocrats in Tunisia and Egypt, Secretary Hillary Clinton pledged to continue U.S. efforts to weaken censorship in countries with repressive governments like China and Iran. In response, China warned the United States to not meddle in internal affairs of other countries, consistent with its usual response to foreign objections of its media repression. Experts say criticism coming from outside China has little effect on its policy.

All inbound data from foreign Internet sources is filtered through one of three computer centers in Beijing, Shanghai, and Guangzhou.

How Do Journalists Get Around Media Control Measures?

Despite the systematic control of news in China—the U.S. State Department estimates China has between thirty thousand and fifty thousand Internet monitors—editors and journalists find ways to get news past the censors. Some analysts say the primary space for freedom of speech in China is the blogosphere, where journalists use humor and political satire to criticize the Chinese government. Bloggers also spell out Chinese characters phonetically or substitute "similar-sounding innocuous characters" to circumvent censorship tools.

In a February 2011 testimony before the U.S.-China Economic and Security Review Commission, CFR's Economy notes how the Internet has increasingly become a means for Chinese citizens to ensure official accountability and rule of law. She also notes the growing importance of social network sites like Twitter as a political force inside China despite government restrictions on them.

In August 2009, Chinese web users won a rare victory over Internet censorship, as China "indefinitely postponed" the installment of censorship software dubbed as the Green Dam Youth Escort, which would systematically block certain websites on all new computers, after an enormous public outcry from Chinese Internet users and foreign computer manufacturers.

China has an estimated 420 million Internet users, and opinions differ on how deeply the Internet is revolutionizing the Chinese media landscape. Some news reports illuminate the difficulty of censoring the Internet as stories slip through government information firewalls.

Inside China, the debate over media censorship continues.

Bob Dietz, Asia program coordinator for the Committee to Protect Journalists, predicts press freedom "will expand to meet the needs and demands not just of the government but of the society." Chinese media broke the news about official suppression of information about the 2003 SARS outbreak in Beijing. Similarly, after toxic chemicals leaked into a river and contaminated drinking water in the northeast city of Harbin in 2005, newspapers and websites criticized government response, demanded greater transparency, and posted photos of area residents stockpiling bottled water.

But Pottinger counters that such evaluations "have been proved wrong by the Chinese government." He adds: "They've cleared pretty significant obstacles in the past in order to institute effective censorship and self-censorship."

Since 2010, Internet users are required to register with their real names before inputting a comment on a chat room or discussion forum. Such legislation chips away at the anonymity that has fostered the freer criticism in recent years and may foreshadow broad and deep Internet controls to come, say some analysts.

But inside China, the debate over media censorship continues. Chinese premier Wen Jiabao's statements in favor of freedom of speech in 2010 were censored within China, yet ignited a great deal of commentary on China's web. It even prompted retired Communist Party officials to publish a letter calling for press freedom. But Columbia University professor Andrew Nathan cautioned: "It's impossible to know exactly what Wen means . . . he probably envisions a great deal less reform and a great deal less human rights than we would think such words imply."

Viewpoint 3

No Free Press in Iraq

Dahr Jamail

In the following viewpoint, Dahr Jamail reports that there is little media freedom in Iraq. Jamail interviews numerous journalists who all claim that freedom of the press is almost nonexistent and that journalists face more dangers now than ever. Jamail claims that contrary to President Barack Obama's praise for press freedom in Iraq, journalists themselves report that the situation has worsened since the United States pulled out of Iraq. Jamail is an independent American reporter based in Doha, Qatar.

As you read, consider the following questions:

1. According to Jamail, what Iraqi journalist and radio show host was assassinated in September 2011?
2. The author says that Iraq's Society for Defending Press Freedom filed an appeal against the "journalists' rights law" for what reason?
3. Jamail quotes a journalist who says that the dangerous situation for journalists has gotten worse since the withdrawal of US forces for what reason?

Attacks on both local and international journalists across Iraq have not stopped to this day, finds Al Jazeera.

Baghdad, Iraq—Iraq has been one of the deadliest countries in the world for journalists since 2003.

Dahr Jamail, "No Free Press in Iraq," Al Jazeera English, January 10, 2012.

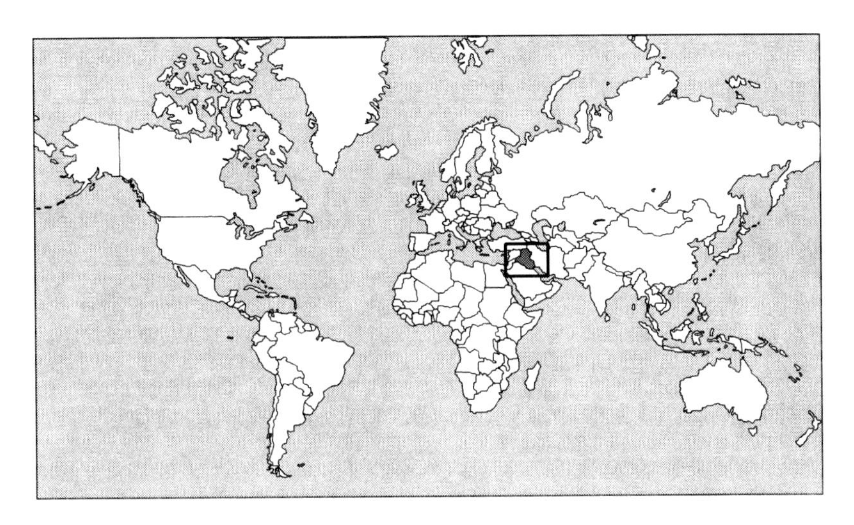

While scores of newspapers and media outlets blossomed across Baghdad following the removal of Saddam Hussein's regime in the spring of 2003, the media renaissance was also met with attacks on both local and international journalists across the country—that have not stopped to this day.

Iraq was the deadliest country in the world for journalists every year from 2003 to 2008, the third deadliest in 2009, and the second deadliest in 2010 and 2011, according to the Committee to Protect Journalists (CPJ).

CPJ documents 150 journalists killed in Iraq since 2003, a number, as high as it is, which pales in comparison to that logged by the group BRussells Tribunal (BT).

Iraq was the deadliest country in the world for journalists every year from 2003 to 2008, the third deadliest in 2009, and the second deadliest in 2010 and 2011.

Logging the name, date, incident description, and source when available, BT reports that 341 Iraqi journalists and media workers have been killed since the invasion.

Adding to the overt physical risks from a dangerous security situation and threats of kidnapping, Iraqi journalists have told Al Jazeera that they now face threats from the Iraqi government itself, led by Prime Minister Nouri al-Maliki.

Adnan Hussein, the editor in chief and deputy director of Iraq's *Al-Mada* newspaper, one of the largest in the country, wrote an article about then prime minister Ibrahim al-Jaafari in 2006.

"I mentioned that he talked too much, so I received an e-mail from one of his supporters," Hussein explained at his office in Baghdad. "The e-mail said: 'If you are in Baghdad we will kill you and throw you in the garbage like the dogs.'"

"So how is our situation?" Hussein asked. "Certainly we are afraid. I give you this example, and it still exists today."

Atmosphere of Fear

On September 8, 2011, Iraqi journalist Hadi al-Mahdi was shot in his Baghdad home by assailants using pistols with silencers. Mahdi had hosted a thrice-weekly radio show covering social and political issues, including government corruption, bribery and sectarianism.

On his Facebook page, Mahdi had regularly organised pro-democracy demonstrations and publicised threats he had received. Having become afraid for his safety, two months before his murder, Mahdi had stepped down from his radio show.

"The killing of Hadi al-Mahdi created an atmosphere of fear," Hussein said of the death of his colleague.

He explained that the Maliki government claimed to have recently passed a law that provided greater protections to Iraqi journalists, but that instead "the law limits our work and does not guarantee our rights".

"Journalists here are now working in the streets naked," he said. "They have no rights and no protections. Journalists cannot work and cover what needs to be covered because they are too exposed."

One of Hussein's colleagues recently accused an Iraqi military spokesman of being a hypocrite in one of his columns, and the spokesman filed a lawsuit against their paper for $6m compensation.

"I returned to Iraq one year ago [after working as the managing editor of *Asharq Alawsat* newspaper in London] to find a bad situation, because of the political situation," Hussein concluded. "But now I feel it will worsen. The Iraqi government is not operating within any rules."

Oday Hattem, chairman of Iraq's Society for Defending Press Freedom, agrees.

Hattem, who was arrested twice by Saddam Hussein's regime for publishing articles that offended the government, knows firsthand about media repression.

"There is no freedom to work in journalism here—if we compare the journalism in Iraq with the West," Hattem told Al Jazeera.

The large number of media outlets available in the country today, "does not necessarily mean there is freedom of the press, because every paper or TV channel belongs to a political party", he said.

If a journalist reports critically "that means this journalist will lose his life".

Hattem believes the laws of journalism from Saddam's era continue to prevent Iraqi journalists from criticising the government, and the fact that religious parties each have their own militia means they, too, are not to be criticised.

According to Hattem, if a journalist reports critically "that means this journalist will lose his life".

Like Hussein, Hattem sees the situation worsening on all fronts.

"The political and freedom of speech situations are both descending," he said. "Maliki launched an attack on freedom

Journalist Safety in Iraq, 2011

In 2011 Iraq remained one of the most dangerous countries in the world to work as a journalist. Armed groups and unknown assailants killed at least five journalists and one media worker, according to the New York–based Committee to Protect Journalists. Journalists also contended with emboldened Iraqi and KRG [Kurdistan Regional Government] security forces.

"World Report 2012: Iraq,"
Human Rights Watch, 2012. www.hrw.org.

of speech in February 2010, when he arrested tens of journalists and human rights activists after the beginning of demonstrations in Baghdad."

US president Barack Obama, during a December 12, 2011, press conference with Iraq's prime minister Nouri al-Maliki, had nothing but high praise for the state of press freedom in Maliki's Iraq:

> So we're partnering to strengthen the institutions upon which Iraq's democracy depends—free elections, a vibrant press, a strong civil society, professional police and law enforcement that uphold the rule of law, an independent judiciary that delivers justice fairly, and transparent institutions that serve all Iraqis.

Three days later, Iraq's Society for Defending Press Freedom filed an appeal with Iraq's high federal court against Maliki's government and its "journalists' rights law", which the group said contradicted four articles from Iraq's constitution.

Like most Iraqi journalists Al Jazeera spoke with, Hattem also received threats through what he said were "departments of the government".

"I have had to change my address several times, and in 2008, my six-year-old daughter was kidnapped," he explained.

Hattem received a death threat in February 2011 which caused him to leave the country for 30 days, "and a lot of my colleagues have left journalism because they have received threats from Shia parties and their militias".

"In November 2011, there was another attempt to kidnap my daughter from in front of school," Hattem said, adding that Maliki and his government are "controlling the media more now than even under Saddam".

"After 2003, we hoped for full freedom of the press as it is in the West," he added. "But the US does not want Iraq to be a democratic country. The spine of democracy is freedom of the press, but since 2003, the US forces never lifted a finger to stop violations against the press and freedom of journalists."

'You Will Be Arrested or Assassinated'

Yasser Faisal from Fallujah has worked as a freelance cameraman for Reuters since 2002, both in and out of Iraq.

He feels that working as a journalist in Iraq today is more difficult than it was under Saddam Hussein's regime.

"If you want to search for the truth about something and this thing is against the interests of the government, you will be either arrested or assassinated," he told Al Jazeera.

Faisal said, after the withdrawal of US forces, "the situation has become even more dangerous" because "there are no international organisations or laws that can protect you, so you can only work if you have contacts or relations with the Iraqi army or police".

He points to the fact that, like every other journalist Al Jazeera spoke with, any time Iraqi security forces are around, journalists are not allowed to take pictures or film, and censorship even within hospitals is alive and well.

Of the new law that supposedly protects Iraqi journalists, Faisal said simply, "it is not effective".

Ibrahim al-Jassim, a reporter for the Al-Masar satellite channel in Iraq, also pointed to the militia of the political parties as part of the problem Iraqi journalists face.

Any time Iraqi security forces are around, journalists are not allowed to take pictures or film, and censorship even within hospitals is alive and well.

"We have many difficulties here," he said, while standing nearby Baghdad's busy Saadoun Street. "These are all dependent on the security situation."

Jassim believes that the targeting of Iraqi journalists is happening "because of the Iraqi political parties not wanting the truth out. Our job is to seek the truth, and nobody here wants the truth to come out".

A 2011 report by Human Rights Watch on freedom of expression in Iraq confirms this: "In 2010, Iraq remained one of the most dangerous countries in the world to work as a journalist. Extremists and unknown assailants continue to kill media workers and bomb their bureaus. . . ."

Many Difficulties

Ahmed Rehayma, office director at the Society for Defending Press Freedom in Iraq, again points to the government for the root of the current problems facing Iraqi journalists.

"This pressure from the government has happened to all of us," he explained. "It's a fact we cannot deny."

Of his reporting for the *Azzaman* newspaper up until four months ago, he said that he always pursued the truth, but that the government is "most certainly putting up obstacles".

He pointed to a story he wrote on how bomb detection devices used by the Iraqi military at checkpoints don't really work.

"The Ministry of Interior tried to make me look like a troublemaker for doing this story," he explained. "They stopped us on that story."

Rehayma told of another instance where he was reporting on a fire and an Iraqi policeman made him delete his photos, and then became physically abusive.

"We know plenty of journalists who have horrible stories," he said. "We see Maliki consolidating power and this concerns us, as it will make things hard for the media. Our media is in trouble now."

VIEWPOINT 4

Media Controls in Iran Are Extremely Repressive

Amnesty International

In the following viewpoint, Amnesty International argues that despite criticism, undue restrictions on media freedom in Iran continue. Amnesty International claims that for decades Iran has had laws that restrict freedom of expression in newspapers, television, and radio; and now such laws are being extended to new technology such as the Internet and text messaging. Amnesty International is a worldwide movement of people who campaign for internationally recognized human rights to be respected and protected for everyone.

As you read, consider the following questions:

1. According to the author, some publications in Iran have been banned under what 1960 law?
2. Amnesty International claims that Iran's cyber police are said to exist for what purpose?
3. According to the author, under the 2008 law on audio-visual crimes, what two punishments can result from producing obscene material?

Amnesty International, "'We Are Ordered to Crush You': Expanding Repression of Dissent in Iran," 2012, pp. 11–14. AI Index: MDE 13/002/2012.

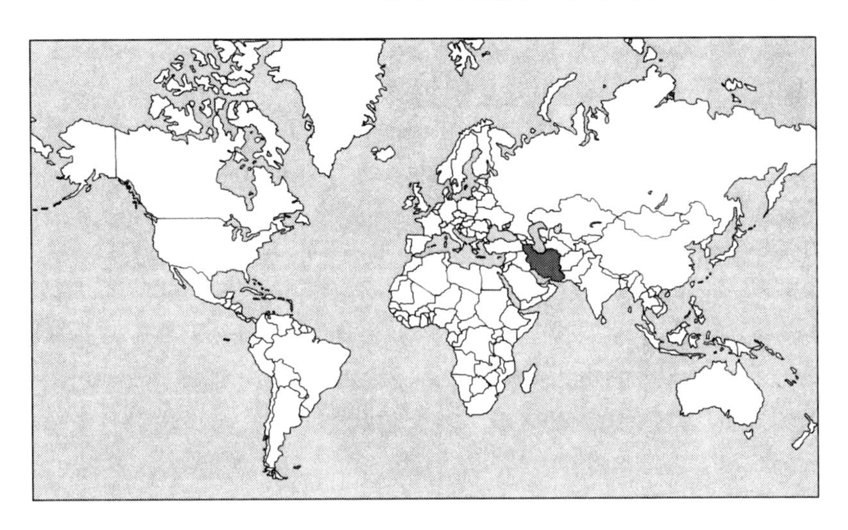

Legislation passed since the 1979 [Iranian] revolution has imposed undue restrictions on the peaceful exercise of the rights to freedom of expression, assembly and association—particularly the 1981 press law, the penal code, the labour code, and the law on political parties, societies, political and guild associations, and Islamic or recognized minority religious associations (political parties law).

Restrictions on Freedom of Expression

Amnesty International has for years been documenting violations of human rights relating to these laws, which have also been criticised by other international human rights monitors such as the UN [United Nations] Human Rights Committee. The UN special rapporteur on the promotion and protection of the right to freedom of opinion and expression has also highlighted his concern at the numerous provisions in the penal code and the press law which restrict freedom of opinion and expression.

In a report published in December 2001, Amnesty International presented and illustrated in detail its concerns about laws which curtail the right to freedom of expression. Since then, the violations detailed in that report have continued unabated. The Iranian authorities continue to ban independent television and radio stations and the use of satellite dishes, on occasion jamming satellite broadcasts from abroad. They have banned books and restricted the paper supply for certain publishers which makes it difficult for them to publish their books. Publications have been banned, mostly temporarily by the Press Supervisory Board, pending decisions by the courts. Some are said to have been closed under the 1960 Preventive Restraint Act. Newspapers are provided with regulations over what they can and cannot publish on certain issues, and journalists and commentators have been targeted for arrest. Countless other Iranians have been harassed and persecuted for expressing their views, whether in print or orally.

However, the Iranian authorities have been particularly concerned at the rise of the Internet over the last decade or more, and the potential it has for people to freely express their views.

Newspapers are provided with regulations over what they can and cannot publish on certain issues, and journalists and commentators have been targeted for arrest.

In common with other repressive governments, the Iranian authorities have gradually been putting in place an array of legal and other measures intended to limit access to the Internet from Iran and to penalise people writing on websites or personal blogs. Additionally, the post-election unrest of 2009 showed the world exactly how powerful a tool social media such as Facebook and Twitter could be both in organizing protests and in reporting on human rights violations committed when protests are repressed. The authorities have taken further measures since then to prevent people in Iran from using such tools to organize dissent. . . .

Iran's Penal Code and Press Code

New measures taken to limit the right of everyone in Iran to exercise their right of expression are rooted in long-standing policy and practice. Iran's penal code, press code and other regulations have provided the basis for the decades-long censorship of newspaper articles; the banning of newspapers; and the vetting of factual and fictional literature, television, plays and film and forms of pictorial art. The press code was amended in April 2009 to cover the material published on the Internet but other legal measures . . . impose even more intrusive restrictions.

Individuals who write in newspapers or websites or who give interviews to the media may be charged under the press code and penal code with "offences" such as "spreading propaganda against the system", "insulting officials", "spreading lies with intent to harm state security" or occasionally "corruption on earth" or "enmity against God".

Iran's various and often parallel security bodies can now scrutinize activists as they use personal computers in the privacy of their homes.

In recent years, a shadowy "Cyber Army", reportedly linked to the Revolutionary Guards [Army of the Guardians of the Islamic Revolution], has carried out attacks on websites at home and abroad, such as against the sites of Twitter and Voice of America. In January 2012, the Police Chief Brigadier General Esmail Ahmadi-Moghaddam announced that the cyber police, established a year before and intended "to confront Internet crimes and counter social networks that spread 'espionage and riots'", was now operational throughout the country.

The Law and New Technology

In August 2011, the minister of culture and Islamic guidance said that the cabinet was preparing a comprehensive public media bill which would bring SMS [short message service, or text] messages and CDs, as well as weblogs or other websites, under the sole remit of the press law. In January 2012, the cyber police issued new regulations requiring owners of Internet cafés to install CCTV [closed-circuit television] cameras and to register the identity and contact details of users before allowing them to use their computers. Such information must be stored for six months and provides yet one more way for security forces to monitor the activities of activists.

Since 2001, the Iranian authorities have gradually increased measures to control Iranians' access to the outside world via electronic means and media. They have restricted bandwidth and are developing state-run servers, specific Internet protocols (IPs), Internet service providers (ISPs) and search engines.

Countless websites, including international and domestic social networking sites, are blocked, as is the www.amnesty.org website of Amnesty International. Many Iranians use proxy hosts and filter-busting programmes to access sites abroad, but increasingly even these are blocked. Providing such software or training in how to use it is a criminal offence.

Iranian officials have stated that they intend to establish a state-wide intranet that conforms to "Islamic principles", which will run in parallel to the World Wide Web and will "replace it in Muslim countries in the region". It appears that by this measure they may be intending in the future to shut off the access of most people in Iran to the global Internet.

Since 2001, the Iranian authorities have gradually increased measures to control Iranians' access to the outside world via electronic means and media.

Monitoring by Officials

Commercial ISPs in Iran that offer Internet connectivity to the public are required to connect via the state-controlled Telecommunication Company of Iran (TCI) which facilitates state control. The authorities also require ISPs to record access to sites by users. Recently issued instructions require Internet cafés to keep detailed data regarding users' identities and the sites they visit for six months.

Moreover, the authorities jam foreign satellite transmissions into the country and access to information is also restricted by the confiscation of satellite dishes, which are illegal in Iran.

The security forces closely monitor fixed line and mobile telephone services, and people who live in Iran routinely assume that their line is tapped and adapt their speech accordingly. SMS services have been reported to have been occasionally blocked, particularly during times and locations where mass demonstrations have been expected.

The 2008 law on audio-visual crimes, amending an earlier version, provides for flogging and the death penalty for the producers of "obscene" products; producers of such products "intended for sexual abuse"; and the principal agents in the production of those products, on the grounds that they are "corrupt on earth". Under article 4, persons who use such products to blackmail others "to fornicate with them" will be charged with rape—for which there is a mandatory death sentence—under the penal code provisions criminalizing adultery and fornication.

More restrictions on freedom of expression were imposed under the 2009 law on cyber crimes which replicated many of the restrictions placed on freedom of expression in the penal code and press law, making it clear that these laws do apply to Internet and electronic publications.

Viewpoint 5

Media Restrictions in the Gambia Threaten Fair Elections

Article 19

In the following viewpoint, Article 19 argues that the most recent presidential election in the Republic of the Gambia, or the Gambia, illustrates that the country continues to fail to respect freedom of expression and freedom of the media. Article 19 contends that the short campaign cycle and dominance of the media by the ruling party call into question the fairness of the election. In addition, the author notes that journalists continue to be silenced by the ruling party. Article 19 works worldwide to protect the rights of freedom of expression and information as fundamental human rights central to freedom and democracy.

As you read, consider the following questions:

1. According to the author, how many candidates ran against the incumbent Yahya Jammeh in the 2001 presidential election?
2. How many days are presidential candidates in the Gambia allowed to campaign, according to the viewpoint?
3. How many times were key members of the Gambia Press Union detained without warrant between July and October of 2011, according to Article 19?

Article 19, "The Gambia: Freedom of Expression Continued Casualty," Statement, December 16, 2011. www.article19.org.

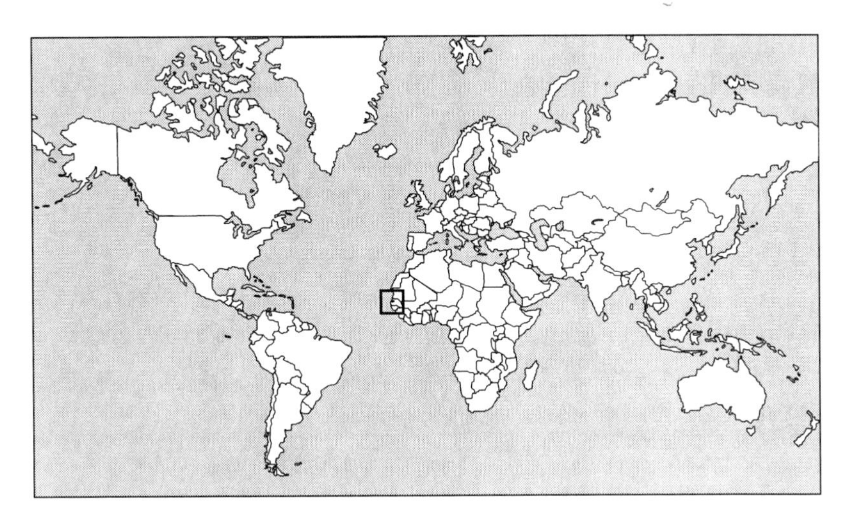

On the occasion of the seven-year anniversary of the killing of renowned Gambian editor, Deyda Hydara, Article 19 remains increasingly concerned at the continuous critical situation of freedom of expression in the Gambia [officially known as the Republic of the Gambia]. The situation has been particularly critical following the November 2011 general election, confirming the president, Yahya Jammeh, remains in power for the fourth term under circumstances that many observers have described as intimidating and falling short of international standards. The electoral process has confirmed the lack of progress in promoting, protecting and fulfilling human rights and basic freedoms in the Gambia, including freedom of expression and freedom of the media.

On 25 November 2011, the Gambian president Yahya Jammeh extended his 17-year government by an additional five years. Jammeh has won the last three consecutive presidential elections of 1996, 2001 and 2007 as leader of the APRC [Alliance for Patriotic Reorientation and Construction]. President Jammeh initially assumed power in a military coup in 1994.

The 2011 election was an opportunity for Gambians to choose their president for the next five years. It was contested by three candidates including: the incumbent, President Yahya

Jammeh from APRC; lawyer, Ousainou Darboe from the United Democratic Party (UDP); and Hamat Bah who resigned from his original party the National Reconciliation Party (NRP) to stand as an independent candidate backed by four political parties under the recently created United Front.

The electoral process has confirmed the lack of progress in promoting, protecting and fulfilling human rights and basic freedoms in the Gambia, including freedom of expression and freedom of the media.

Amid the controversies over the results announced by the Independent Electoral Commission (IEC), Jammeh has already declared that he will stand for the 2016 presidential elections.

The Gambia has been repeatedly criticised for its human rights record by international and regional bodies. Over the past years, the African Commission on Human and Peoples' Rights (ACHPR) has made a series of recommendations and resolutions calling for the Gambian government to respect freedom of expression. These have not had a significant impact. Similarly, during the Universal Periodic Review before the UN Human Rights Council in 2010, the Gambia government rejected recommendations to address with more determination the critical situation of freedom of expression and the security of journalists and human rights defenders. For similar reasons, the Economic Community of West African States (ECOWAS) officially declined to observe the presidential elections in the country.

Principles of Free and Fair Elections

As a party to a number of international and regional human rights instruments, the Gambia is obliged to uphold the right to freedom of expression, and principles of free and fair elections should guide its political life.

Article 19 is concerned about numerous reports indicating that the electoral process in the Gambia was not conducted with due respect to the stated principles and there is fear that the upcoming popular consultations to be held in the Gambia will suffer the same undemocratic environment if no proper action is taken.

According to international standards on freedom of expression and elections, candidates or political parties should be given equal airtime on public and private media in the campaign period. They should not use their incumbency or other privileged status such as their financial position to influence the campaign period and the overall electoral process. The media should be impartial in the treatment of political parties and candidates during the electoral campaign and should participate in the voters' education and exercise their duty without fear of reprisal from anybody be it public or private.

The Electoral Process in the Gambia

Article 19 believes that the electoral process in the Gambia fell short of these benchmarks and was not conducted with due respect to international or regional standards for the following reasons.

- According to the IEC electoral calendar, the Gambia's electoral process consists of three separate elections (24 November—presidential elections; first quarter of 2012—parliamentary elections; and first quarter of 2013—local government elections). For the November election, the IEC has only allowed candidates for the concluded presidential elections to campaign for 11 days. The extremely short duration of the campaign for an important election like this was criticised by many observers and the opposition. It is a particular issue in the Gambian context where the opposition candidates have very little opportunity to share their perspective and explain their manifestos to the public outside of the official campaigning period.

- Observers and the opposition have consistently denounced for several years the inequality of the coverage of the activities of political parties in the public media. The ruling Alliance for Patriotic Reorientation and Construction (APRC) of President Jammeh exercises complete control over the state media so that almost no diverse or opposition views are broadcasted. This problem was particularly acute during the pre-election campaign. The predominantly pro-government nature of public media coverage negatively affected the public's access to diverse views. Incumbent or ruling party candidates had much greater visibility by the public media and, therefore, held a considerable electoral advantage over their political opponents.
- Many violations of international principles on freedom of expression and election have been noted by independent observers, including the Commonwealth Election [Observation] Missions. They have noted various problems through which the opposition candidates' ability to campaign were hampered. For example, security officers and civil servants openly demonstrated support to the incumbent president. Uniformed military personnel participated in the APRC rally held in Banjul [the capital of the Gambia] on Saturday 19 November 2011. Three military trucks were also seen transporting youths wearing the party colour and emblem of the APRC in Churchill's Town on 23 November 2011. Public officials openly campaigned for the APRC ruling party, including governors and their officers. There were attempts to prevent

some candidates from holding rallies in some parts of the country. The IEC itself was obliged to denounce the practice in a statement of 17 November 2011 condemning openly these undemocratic behaviours. Many local organisations were blocked from independent, observatory roles. There have been numerous instances of unequal treatment of candidates and political parties in the media. For instance, the private newspaper the *Observer* reported that public institutions, such as the Ministry of Petroleum, were donating campaign T-shirts to the APRC.

The ruling Alliance for Patriotic Reorientation and Construction . . . exercises complete control over the state media so that almost no diverse or opposition views are broadcasted.

The Treatment of Journalists

As already noted, the Gambia is notorious for being a repressive country that limits freedom of expression and its intolerance of journalists and human rights advocates.

Journalists who do not follow the ruling party's line have faced harassments and intimidation, arbitrary arrest from security agencies, as well as physical violence. Outside of the campaign period, whoever openly challenges or criticises the government is likely to be charged with sedition or treason and jailed. Due to this repressive environment, self-censorship of journalists and media owners is a regular practice. Such threats have escalated since the killing of journalist Deyda Hydara in 2004 and the disappearance of Chief [Ebrima] Manneh in 2006. These two major cases have had a significant chilling effect on professional journalism in the Gambia. Despite several years having passed since these incidents, there have been no independent investigations and no convictions for these crimes, and there has been no political will to bring perpetrators to justice. In a November 2011 interview to BBC, President Jammeh publicly stated that the killing was not a matter of specific concern in the Gambia.

Journalists, opposition leaders, media professionals and common citizens are subjected to harsh laws (such as sedition, defamation and offences of giving false information to public officials) that aim at suppressing freedom of speech. For example,

- In 2009, President Jammeh released a statement that threatened to kill human rights workers. In 2009, several members of the Gambia Press Union were arrested and charged with sedition.
- Since June 2011, Dr. [Amadou] Scattred Janneh, a former minister of information, has been detained and facing prosecution on treason charges for printing and distributing T-shirts reading "Coalition For Change: End Dictatorship now". Among his co-accused are the free expression advocate and former president of the Gambia Press Union, Ndey Tapha Sosseh.
- On 5 July 2011, journalist Nanama Keita, a former sports editor of the *Daily Observer* newspaper, was arrested and charged with giving false information to a public officer on the back of a petition he had made to the office of the president claiming wrongful dismissal as deputy editor in chief and head of the sports desk. In the petition, he had also alleged that the managing director of the Observer Company had engaged in financial malpractice. Nanama Keita fled the country in September 2011 while the proceedings were still pending. Subsequently in November 2011, Saikou Ceesay, a journalist with the *Daily News* and an executive member of the Gambia Press Union, . . . was arrested and summoned to pay a fine of a hun-

dred thousand dalasi (around 3,500 USD). He was ultimately freed on bail paid by the Gambia Press Union.

- From July 2011 to October 2011, the key executive members of the Gambia Press Union were arrested, detained and questioned three times by the police without warrant.
- On 16 September 2011, a magistrates' court in Banjul convicted and sentenced Dodou Sanneh, a former reporter with the Gambia Radio and Television Services (GRTS), to a fine of five hundred dalasi in default to serve six months in jail after he was found guilty on accusation of giving false information to a public officer. The case originated when Sanneh filed a petition with the office of the president of the Gambia against his dismissal from the GRTS.
- In August 2011, the National Intelligence Agency put in place an injunction on Teranga FM—an independent community radio station—prohibiting local language broadcasting. This inhibited many listeners' access to public information and is a good example of the lack of tolerance of diverse viewpoints and the desire of the authorities to keep citizens uninformed.

Journalists, opposition leaders, media professionals and common citizens are subjected to harsh laws . . . that aim at suppressing freedom of speech.

Following election victory, President Jammeh has continued to threaten journalists and human rights defenders. On 28 November 2011, Gambian election day, he declared that he would not reconsider his position on the treatment of the Gambian media because, "journalists are less than 1% of the population . . . if anybody expects me to allow less than 1% of the population to destroy 99% of the population, you are in the wrong place." . . .

In Article 19's view, the situation of freedom of expression in the Gambia is likely to become more critical in the coming years. Article 19 will therefore continue to monitor the situation in the Gambia and provide support to journalists, human rights advocates and civil society and those whose rights are violated and call for the mobilisation of stakeholders to work toward a reform of the repressive environment under which journalists and civil society advocates operate.

Periodical and Internet Sources Bibliography

The following articles have been selected to supplement the diverse views presented in this chapter.

Amnesty International	"Freedom of Expression Under Fire: Briefing to the Hungarian Government on the New Media Legislation," March 18, 2011. www.amnesty.org.
Article 19	"Western Europe: Freedom of Expression in Retreat in 2009," December 21, 2009. www.article19.org.
Denis Barnabas	"Uganda: The Shrinking Space for Freedom of Speech," *Foreign Policy*, February 3, 2012.
Peter Foster	"Leading Chinese Dissident Claims Freedom of Speech Worse than Before Olympics," *Telegraph* (UK), April 27, 2009.
Human Rights Watch	"A Media Minefield: Increased Threats to Freedom of Expression in Uganda," May 2, 2010. www.hrw.org.
Renee Lewis	"Somalia, the Deadliest Place in Africa for Journalists," Human Rights House Network, January 10, 2011. http://humanrightshouse.org.
Maria Lipman	"Rethinking Russia: Freedom of Expression Without Freedom of the Press," *Journal of International Affairs*, Spring/Summer 2010.
Navi Pillay	"Twenty Years on from the Windhoek Declaration: Freedom of the Press in a Changed World," United Nations, May 3, 2011. www.un.org.
Keith B. Richburg	"In China, Microblogging Sites Become Free-Speech Platform," *Washington Post*, March 27, 2011.

Chapter 3

The Right to Due Process

VIEWPOINT 1

In the West Bank, Administrative Measures Threaten Due Process

Mordechai Kremnitzer and Lina Saba

In the following viewpoint, Mordechai Kremnitzer and Lina Saba argue that criminal procedures rather than military legal orders are the preferable way to deal with lawbreakers in Judea and Samaria, an area also known as the West Bank. The authors contend that restraining or incarcerating suspects without due process is unacceptable for both Jewish and Palestinian residents. Kremnitzer is vice president of research at the Israel Democracy Institute and a professor emeritus in the Faculty of Law at the Hebrew University of Jerusalem. Saba is a research assistant at the Israel Democracy Institute.

As you read, consider the following questions:

1. According to the authors, does international law that applies to territories under military occupation allow administrative detention?
2. In comparing administrative measures and criminal proceedings, which do the authors say are directed toward the future and which toward the past?

Mordechai Kremnitzer and Lina Saba, "Restraining Orders Should Alarm Settlers," *The Jerusalem Post*, January 11, 2012.

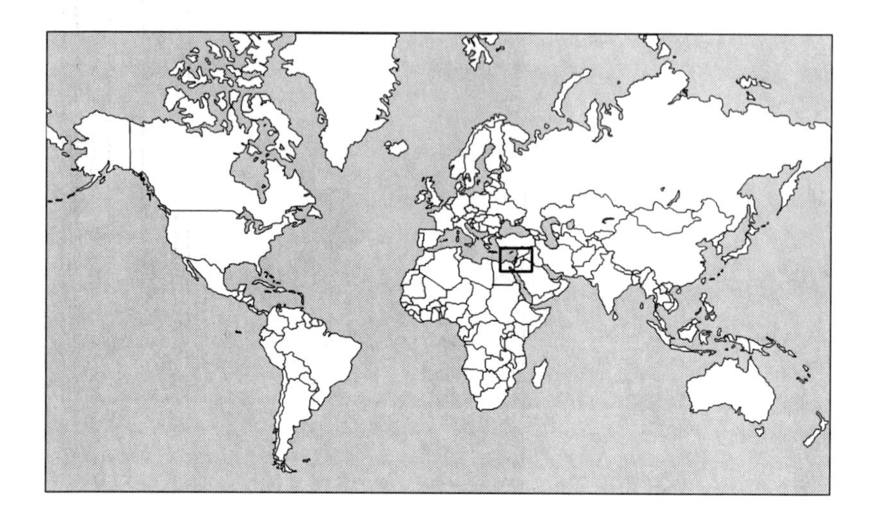

3. The authors cite the B'Tselem organization as claiming that as of November 2011, how many Palestinians were being held in administrative detention?

Maj. Gen. [Major General] Avi Mizrahi's administrative restraining orders against 12 right-wing activists bar them from Judea and Samaria [the West Bank] for periods ranging from three to nine months. These orders were issued at the recommendation of the Israel Security Agency (Shin Bet).

According to the IDF [Israel Defense Forces] statement, the Central Command's orders were issued based on information recently gathered by the ISA [Israel Security Agency] which indicated that "the group of extremists has been involved in leading, directing and executing violent and clandestine activity targeting Palestinian residents of Judea and Samaria and security forces operating in the area, therefore endangering lives and disrupting public order."

The Legal Basis for Administrative Measures

The legal basis for issuing these orders is not Israeli law but rather military law, which applies to Judea and Samaria as a result of the IDF's control of these areas, and on international law. The international law that applies to territories under military occupation specifically allows administrative detention.

According to the regulation pertaining to security provisions, a military commander who believes that a restraining order is necessary on compelling security grounds is authorized to issue an order removing a person from a particular area. This regulation does not require the commander to conduct a preliminary procedure, nor does it require him to give the suspect an opportunity to be heard.

The order may be appealed to a committee appointed by the president of the Military Court of Appeals. This committee may deviate from the rules of evidence and is also not bound by the rules of procedure. For security reasons, it is also entitled to accept evidence while preventing the restrained person and his legal representative from examining the evidence.

There is no doubt that there is immediate and critical need to enforce the law in the territories and to prevent violence against Palestinians and against Israeli security forces. The question, however, is what measures are appropriate for achieving this important goal, since the end does not justify all means.

The Superiority of Criminal Procedures

There is no doubt that the proper way of dealing with lawbreakers is through the criminal process, since criminal procedures guarantee that the suspect's right to due process will be protected, and allows sanctions against people only after they have been proven guilty of a crime beyond a reasonable doubt.

Administrative measures, in contrast, are taken on the basis of the provisions of the executive branch without criminal charges being filed, without trial and without judicial decision. They are also generally imposed under a heavy veil of secrecy, such that suspects are not able to deal with the alleged evidence against them and defend themselves against the allegations against them. This situation violates the right to due process and the human dignity of the suspects. It also does not allow a thorough examination of the allegations.

Administrative measures are ostensibly preventive measures directed toward the future, while criminal proceedings are conducted for acts done in the past. In fact, what generally leads to the imposition of administrative measures is difficultly in proving that a criminal offense was committed, usually because of secret evidence.

There is no doubt that the proper way of dealing with lawbreakers is through the criminal process, since criminal procedures guarantee that the suspect's right to due process will be protected.

The Problem with Administrative Measures

If we examine the long-standing reality in Judea and Samaria, it is hard to avoid the conclusion that there has been an ongoing failure to enforce the law when crimes have been committed by Jews in the occupied territories. Against this background, it is difficult to accept the use of administrative measures, unless it is as a temporary measure that will be in effect only until the root of this failure can be addressed and it is possible to conduct criminal proceedings in such cases.

The type of evidence that is admissible is also not the will of heaven; rather, it is controlled by humans. In a situation in which there is no "arrangement" of restraining orders or administrative detention, the system would probably recruit and handle agents in a manner that would allow agents to be exposed by being brought as witnesses. Information that is inad-

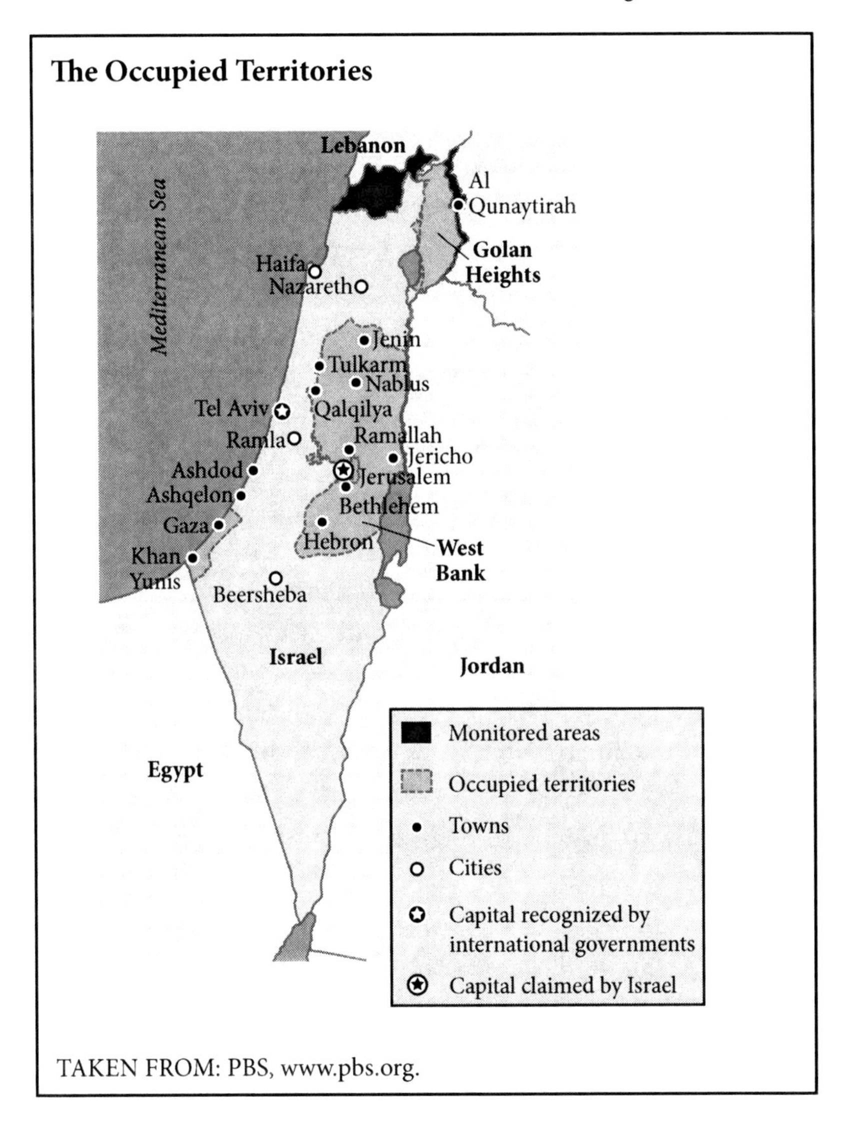

TAKEN FROM: PBS, www.pbs.org.

missible intelligence information at an early stage of the process should serve as the point of departure for an investigation that will yield admissible evidence.

The existence of administrative measures makes life easy for the law enforcement system and creates a disincentive to develop measures that might make administrative measures unnecessary. It is not appropriate, and it is not fair, but it is easy.

In the exceptional cases in which it is not possible to use the standard methods of law enforcement, the authorities must employ the measure that violates human rights the least while still achieving the desired goal. Thus, for example, if it's possible to deal with the danger posed by a suspect by putting him under surveillance, that measure should be adopted.

Anyone who believes that such measures are illegitimate or at least problematic when imposed upon Jews will be hard-pressed to justify their imposition on Palestinians.

Proposed Changes to the Law

Although serving a restraining order is less severe than incarcerating a suspect (administrative detention), it involves a serious blow to the rights of the person who is being removed and a fatal blow to the right to due process.

In order to lessen the impact of restraining orders in cases where there is no recourse but to issue them, a number of changes to the existing law are necessary:

1. A hearing must be held so that the suspect can defend himself.
2. The suspect must be allowed to be assisted by a lawyer who is acceptable to the security authorities, who will have access to the secret evidence.
3. The duration of the restraining order should not exceed what is required by the specific circumstances.

When considering these steps, we must remember that the Palestinians in the territories are living under a regime that employs measures far more extreme than the restraining orders in question, such as administrative detention that can continue for months and even years without trial. According to the B'Tselem organization, as of November 2011, approximately 280 Palestinians were being held in administrative detention.

The administrative restraining orders that were imposed on 12 Jewish suspects serve as an impetus for the Jewish public to consider—as an expression of concern—the measures that are being taken by our governmental authorities as a matter of course against Palestinian residents. Anyone who believes that such measures are illegitimate or at least problematic when imposed upon Jews will be hard-pressed to justify their imposition on Palestinians. Applying them only to Palestinians is not acceptable according to the rule of law.

VIEWPOINT 2

Letter to President Obama: End Detention Without Trial and Close Guantánamo

Kenneth Roth

In the following viewpoint, Kenneth Roth asks President Barack Obama to follow through on his commitment to close the Guantánamo Bay detention camp where Roth claims detainees are denied their due process rights. Roth contends that the detention practices of the United States at Guantánamo Bay violate its own commitment to due process and set a bad example for other countries. He claims that detainees cleared for release or resettlement should be freed and that all detainees not released should be tried in the federal courts. Roth is executive director of Human Rights Watch.

As you read, consider the following questions:

1. According to Roth, what law was recently signed by President Barack Obama that continues to support a military detention system for dealing with terrorism?
2. The Guantánamo Review Task Force of 2009 determined that how many detainees should continue to be detained without charge, according to the author?

Kenneth Roth, "Letter to President Obama: End Detention Without Trial and Close Guantanamo," Human Rights Watch, January 10, 2012.

3. Who is the only former Guantánamo detainee to be transferred to the United States for trial, according to Roth?

Dear President [Barack] Obama:

We write to you on the eve of the tenth anniversary [January 10, 2012] of the detention facility at Guantánamo Bay to urge you to reaffirm your stated commitment to closing Guantánamo by prosecuting detainees in federal court and repatriating and resettling those who will not be prosecuted.

The National Defense Authorization Act

We are deeply disappointed that you chose to sign into law the National Defense Authorization Act (NDAA) despite your administration's repeated threats to veto the bill if it contained detention provisions detrimental to the rule of law and US national security. The new law represents a complete rejection of the vision you outlined for counterterrorism policy when you took office. The final version of the bill, while amended slightly, seeks to upend the effective use of law enforcement for countering terrorism and replace it with a military detention system.

Your signing statement appended to the bill noted a number of deeply problematic areas which you have committed to interpreting in a manner that avoids constitutional conflicts and complies with the laws of war. Yet those problematic areas are the very reason you should have vetoed the bill, and why you must make repeal of those provisions a top priority for your administration this year. As long as the NDAA remains a part of US law, it can be used by future administrations to detain people indefinitely even in circumstances your administration has disavowed. While working towards this goal, we urge you to interpret the provisions in a manner consistent with international human rights and humanitarian law, and to exercise your discretionary powers to use civilian law enforcement tools to prosecute terrorism suspects. We recognize that repeal may be difficult. Nevertheless, we believe the strong bipartisan opposition to the detention provisions of the NDAA made clear that key members of Congress will support any efforts to repeal those provisions that are inconsistent with US values and the rule of law.

Your National Security Strategy explicitly recognizes that the United States' "moral leadership is grounded principally in the power of [its] example." Your National Strategy for Counterterrorism recognizes the importance of adhering to US core values while fighting terrorism, including through the respect for human rights. As the strategy eloquently outlined, "Where terrorists offer injustice, disorder, and destruction, the United States must stand for freedom, fairness, equality, dignity, hope, and opportunity. The power and appeal of our values enables the United States to build a broad coalition to act collectively against the common threat posed by terrorists, further delegitimizing, isolating, and weakening our adversaries." In his speech at Harvard Law School in September 2011, counterterrorism advisor John Brennan affirmed that the guiding principle of all US action is to "uphold the core values that define us as Americans, and that includes adhering to the rule of law."

International Reaction to US Detention Practices

The example set by keeping Guantánamo open undermines the US government's long-standing opposition to similar detention regimes in other countries. Over the years, the US has opposed detention practices that are inconsistent with basic principles of due process, openly criticizing detentions without trial by Saudi Arabia, Pakistan, Malaysia, and China. But such criticisms hold little weight when the US adopts its own indefinite detention regime. Zimbabwe's Robert Mugabe, Russia's Vladimir Putin, Bashar al-Assad of Syria, and Iran's Mahmoud Ahmadinejad have all pointed to Guantánamo to deflect attention from human rights abuses in their own countries. In May 2010 your administration criticized Egypt's extension of a state of emergency that has been continuously in effect since 1981. In responding to that criticism, the Egyptian government explained that its efforts were no different from the United States' failure to close Guantánamo. In December 2011, as part of a campaign to deflect criticism of its own human rights record, Russia criticized the US for, among other things, keeping Guantánamo open.

In the early months of your administration, many governments responded favorably to your stated commitment to closing Guantánamo, including by accepting detainees for resettlement despite the US government's refusal to do the same. But in recent months, in meetings with senior government officials around the world, Human Rights Watch representatives have seen a resumption of criticism leveled against the US by countries with some of the most repressive human rights policies (such as Saudi Arabia, China, Libya under [Muammar] Gaddafi, and Egypt under [Hosni] Mubarak), who feel immune from criticism because the US engages in similar practices and has not held any high-level officials accountable for past abuse.

Despite your stated commitment to closing Guantánamo, in your May 2009 speech at the National Archives you outlined several categories of detainees, including a category of those who allegedly "cannot be prosecuted yet who pose a clear danger to the American people." The Guantánamo Review Task Force ("Task Force") recommended 48 detainees for continued detention without charge (now 46 due to the deaths of two of those detainees). On March 7, 2011, you issued an executive order for the Periodic Review of Individuals Detained at Guantánamo Bay Naval Station Pursuant to the Authorization for Use of Military Force ("Executive Order"). While we have long opposed indefinite detention without trial, we commended your administration for limiting the order to those detainees already at Guantánamo, as we believed it was a signal that your administration remained committed to ending the system of indefinite detention that Guantánamo has come to represent.

The example set by keeping Guantánamo open undermines the US government's long-standing opposition to similar detention regimes in other countries.

We acknowledge that you inherited a complicated problem from the previous administration and that you have committed not to expand the population of detainees at Guantánamo. But we regret both your decision to sign into law the NDAA and thereby potentially expand indefinite detention without trial, and your acceptance of indefinite detention without trial for certain detainees already at Guantánamo, as well as detainees in Afghanistan. While we sincerely hope you will revisit those decisions, including by following through on your statement that you will seek repeal of the rights-infringing provisions of the NDAA, there are also steps we believe you can and should take now to mitigate existing harmful policies.

Improving Due Process Protections for Persons in Indefinite Detention

First, we urge you to improve the process under which the detainees in Guantánamo or Afghanistan can challenge their detention. The Executive Order did provide for some additional process protections for persons currently detained at Guantánamo, but instead of providing for the assistance of counsel at periodic review boards, it provides only for a government-appointed military representative. This is a blatant denial by your administration of basic due process rights—a denial that is already occurring in Afghanistan. As in the so-called administrative review of detention in Afghanistan, detainees subject to the new review process at Guantánamo are to be denied access to classified evidence, even if it is used to justify their continued detention. Further, we note that the Executive Order required the secretary of defense, in consultation with the attorney general, to issue implementing guidelines governing the review process. As the Executive Order required initial review to commence no later than one year from the date of the order, we would expect to see draft guidelines available for public comment soon, in advance of the March 7, 2012, deadline for implementing the order.

Section 1024 of the NDAA requires that a military judge oversee status determinations for persons "who will be held in long-term detention under the law of war pursuant to the Authorization for Use of Military Force." Your signing statement indicates that you interpret section 1024 as granting the secretary of defense broad discretion to decide whether status determinations in Afghanistan are covered by this section. We urge you to find that all status determinations conducted by US forces are covered by the procedures of section 1024; in particular, the determination currently made at the initial detainee review board conducted within 60 days of capture, as well as the biannual reviews conducted thereafter. Further, while section 1024(c) makes the provision of a military judge and lawyer optional for detainees who have access to habeas corpus review (i.e., those currently held at Guantánamo), we urge you to implement procedures guaranteeing all persons held in US military detention access to a lawyer and a judge.

We urge you to improve the process under which the detainees in Guantánamo or Afghanistan can challenge their detention.

Repatriate or Resettle Those Already Recommended for Transfer

Second, you should affirm your commitment to closing Guantánamo by transferring those detainees already cleared for release or resettlement as soon as possible. We understand that your administration found the certification requirement contained in the NDAA for FY11 [fiscal year 2011] to be too onerous to sign. While the NDAA for FY12 contains a similar requirement, it also includes a national security waiver that can be exercised by the secretary of defense. We urge your administration to immediately commence completing the certifications necessary to permit the transfer of the 89 detainees in Guantánamo already cleared for transfer by the Task Force, either through the certification process or the national security waiver. Your decision to impose a moratorium on repatriations to Yemen following the attempted bombing of an airliner by Umar Farouk Abdulmutallab (who has since pleaded guilty in federal court) significantly hampered your ability to close Guantánamo. The moratorium was based on conduct wholly unrelated to that of the dozens of Yemeni detainees cleared for transfer by the Task Force. It paved the way for Congress to act similarly by seeking to prevent repatriations based not on any factors relating to a particular detainee's past conduct but instead on alleged acts of recidivism by citizens of the same nation. We urge you to formally lift this moratorium (independent of any certification requirements related to the NDAA) and exercise your discretion to commence the repatriation to Yemen of Yemeni citizens who have been cleared for transfer by the Task Force.

Reject Use of Military Commissions in Favor of Federal Courts

Third, we believe your decision to resurrect the discredited military commissions was also a major mistake. While your administration worked with Congress to improve the military commissions, they remain an unacceptably flawed alternative to the federal courts. Among other flaws, military commissions retroactively define crimes, admit hearsay evidence that is inadmissible in federal courts, and have ever-changing procedures without the benefit of established precedent. The prosecution of Omar Khadr made the US the first Western nation to prosecute someone for alleged war crimes committed as a child, and because the conduct with which he was charged had never before been considered a violation of the laws of war, his case discredited the entire system. The only case currently pending before the military commissions, that of Abd al-Rahim al-Nashiri, is one in which the prosecution is seeking the death penalty. The prosecution of a capital case will only exacerbate the defects of the military commissions, furthering the denial of a fair trial to the defendant and providing additional fodder to terrorist recruiters, who will proclaim al-Nashiri a martyr if executed.

Prosecution in US federal criminal court remains the most effective way to neutralize and punish terrorists. The Justice Department's protocol for trying Guantánamo detainees recognizes that trial in an Article III court is the preferred option. Nevertheless, the only former Guantánamo detainee to be transferred to the US for trial was Ahmed Ghailani, who faced a preexisting indictment in the Southern District of New York. Congressionally imposed restrictions on the use of funds to transfer detainees to the US operate as an effective ban on federal court trials, at least for this fiscal year. You have twice pledged to work with Congress to repeal those restrictions. We urge you to redouble your efforts and to refuse to sign any further such restrictions into law. Article III courts are the most effective way to prosecute terrorism suspects, and their use is key to maintaining foreign ally support, which is necessary in the fight against terrorism and for the closure of Guantánamo.

While your administration worked with Congress to improve the military commissions, they remain an unacceptably flawed alternative to the federal courts.

Guantánamo is a mistake you inherited. The 171 remaining detainees at Guantánamo are the last of a terrible legacy left by the previous administration. They should be the last people in US custody to ever be subjected to a detention regime that strayed so far from the values and principles embodied in the US Constitution and international law. This regime must be so thoroughly repudiated that no future administration would ever consider reviving it. Statements that your administration will not send additional detainees to Guantánamo, while important, are not enough. You must take firm and decisive action to make clear that future detention in Guantánamo is not an option for this or any future administration.

The last year has seen momentous changes around the world. Ordinary people rose up, largely peacefully, to reject repressive governments and restore, or instill, democratic institutions, particularly in the Arab world. In the past, many have looked to the US for leadership and guidance in the promotion of human rights. But now, instead of seeing adherence to the rule of law and respect for human rights, they see a lack of accountability for past abuse, codification of indefinite detention, and the militarization of law enforcement. Not only are your actions important for upholding fundamental rights in the United States, they also send a message to other nations around the world about what the international community expects of democracies.

We urge you to act on your stated commitment to justice and the rule of law by redoubling your efforts to close Guantánamo once and for all. We call on you to put into practice your statement that you will seek repeal of the rights-infringing provisions of the NDAA and that you will refuse to authorize any further encroachments on the rule of law.

VIEWPOINT 3

Abusive Detention Practices in Afghanistan Are a Growing Problem

Chris Rogers

In the following viewpoint, Chris Rogers argues that there are extensive human rights abuses occurring against detainees in Afghanistan. Rogers claims that a recent report found evidence of widespread torture and mistreatment, and he argues for action by the Afghan government to stop the abuses. Rogers also contends that the international community can put pressure on the Afghan government to make the necessary reforms and restore due process of law. Rogers is a human rights lawyer for the Open Society Foundations specializing in human rights and conflict in Afghanistan and Pakistan.

As you read, consider the following questions:

1. According to Rogers, what action did the International Security Assistance Force (ISAF) take in response to the recent report by the United Nations?
2. What US law prohibits support for foreign security forces engaged in gross violations of human rights, according to the author?

Chris Rogers, "Time to Tackle Torture Is Now," *Foreign Policy*, October 11, 2011.

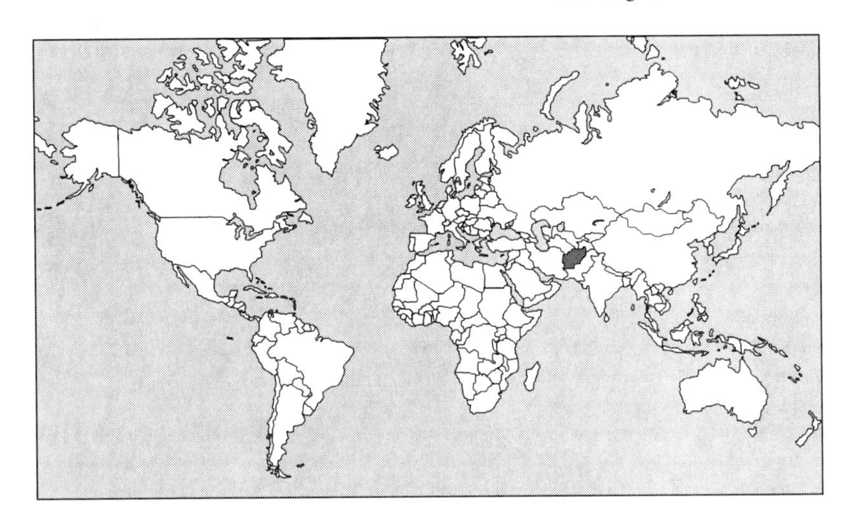

3. What three reasons does Rogers give for thinking that even the most well-designed monitoring systems cannot ensure detainees will be free from torture?

Last year [2010], Qasim, a construction worker from eastern Afghanistan, was detained in a joint US-Afghan raid on his home in Kabul. He eventually ended up in the hands of the National Directorate of Security (NDS), the Afghan intelligence agency. For over a week, Qasim was hung by his arms, taken down only to go the bathroom and pray. Several times a night he was beaten with pipes and electrical cables, his head bashed into walls, and threatened with much worse. After a week and a half, he could no longer walk, not even to bring himself to the bathroom. My organization, Open Society Foundations, and its Afghan partners have interviewed many other Afghans who, like Qasim, have suffered acts of torture at the hands of the NDS, ranging from beatings and burns to electric shock and sexual abuse.

Torture and Mistreatment in Afghanistan

In a groundbreaking report released yesterday [October 10, 2011] by the United Nations Assistance Mission in Afghanistan (UNAMA), the true scope and severity of such abuse is made clear. The UN found evidence of torture and mistreatment in 16 Afghan detention facilities, including electric shocks, hanging detainees from ceilings, beatings, and threat of sexual assault. As a result of the report, the Afghan government dismissed several NDS officials implicated in the report, though it is unclear whether there will be any criminal prosecutions. The International Security Assistance Force (ISAF) has temporarily halted the transfer of ISAF detainees to the 16 facilities.

ISAF's halting of transfers to facilities identified in the UN report is an important first step. The Afghan government's initial response was certainly less positive, but will hopefully improve now that the report has been publicly released. Looking forward, however, there is real concern that the ISAF and Afghan government responses will prove rather superficial and ultimately will fail to fully grapple with the depths of the problem.

One area that the Afghan government and ISAF should prioritize is accountability. Though perhaps politically difficult, accountability for abuses is key and must be pursued vigorously and publicly. The UN report is an opportunity for the right signals to be sent, both within the Afghan justice system as well as to the Afghan public.

The UN found evidence of torture and mistreatment in 16 Afghan detention facilities, including electric shocks, hanging detainees from ceilings, beatings, and threat of sexual assault.

Without sustained efforts on this front, it's likely that even if those Afghan officials who are responsible for abuse are removed, they will only reemerge elsewhere in the justice system or government. Shuffling the problem around only sows the seeds for future abuse and reinforces perceptions of impunity that are at the heart of the Afghan government's struggle for legitimacy.

An independent, external body should be empowered to monitor facilities, receive complaints, and investigate allegations of abuse, with findings and remedial actions made public. Full, unfettered access should also be granted to outside monitors, including the Afghan Independent Human Rights Commission, ICRC [International Committee of the Red Cross], and UNAMA. Those responsible for abuse should not only be removed from their positions, but also subject to criminal prosecution and civil liability.

A Lack of Due Process

The international community can play an important role in ensuring those responsible are truly held to account. Governments should not only apply conventional diplomatic pressure, but should think creatively and ambitiously about how to strengthen accountability. Funding and training as well as military and intelligence relationships with the Afghan government and security forces should all be utilized to ensure those responsible for abuse are held accountable. The US is prohibited by the Leahy Law from supporting foreign security forces which engage in gross violations of human rights.

The pervasive lack of due process also leaves detainees vulnerable to abuse. Detainees and defense lawyers we have interviewed consistently decry Afghan authorities' denial of legal counsel, in addition to preventing family notification or contact. In some cases we documented, defense lawyers have themselves been arrested or harassed simply for contacting their clients. The Afghan government should implement measures to ensure detainees' access to legal counsel and adopt strict rules regarding family notification (just as the Afghan government advocates for in ISAF detentions), while international donors should provide funding to Afghan legal aid or-

Evidence of Torture in Afghanistan

From October 2010 to August 2011, the United Nations Assistance Mission in Afghanistan (UNAMA) interviewed 379 pretrial detainees and convicted prisoners at 47 detention facilities in 22 provinces across Afghanistan. In total, 324 of the 379 persons interviewed were detained by National Directorate of Security (NDS) or Afghan National Police (ANP) forces for national security crimes—suspected of being Taliban fighters, suicide attack facilitators, producers of improvised explosive devices, and others implicated in crimes associated with the armed conflict in Afghanistan. . . .

UNAMA's detention observation found compelling evidence that 125 detainees (46 percent) of the 273 detainees interviewed who had been in NDS detention experienced interrogation techniques at the hands of NDS officials that constituted torture, and that torture is practiced systematically in a number of NDS detention facilities throughout Afghanistan. Nearly all detainees tortured by NDS officials reported the abuse took place during interrogations and was aimed at obtaining a confession or information. In almost every case, NDS officials stopped the use of torture once detainees confessed to the crime of which they were accused or provided the requested information. UNAMA also found that children under the age of 18 years experienced torture by NDS officials.

More than one-third of the 117 conflict-related detainees UNAMA interviewed who had been in ANP detention experienced treatment that amounted to torture or to other cruel, inhuman or degrading treatment.

United Nations Assistance Mission in Afghanistan (UNAMA), "Treatment of Conflict-Related Detainees in Afghan Custody," October 2011.

ganizations to represent conflict-related detainees. Ensuring detainees have their most basic due process rights respected while in detention provides an additional, necessary check on Afghan authorities' power and strengthens transparency and accountability.

For their part, international forces must acknowledge that there are no quick fixes for detainee abuse in Afghanistan. Detainee monitoring, for example, is too often posited as the solution to abuse, although it only focuses on detainees transferred by international forces, not the wider prison population. While monitoring is a potentially important part of protecting detainee rights, international forces must be honest about its practical limitations, and confront the fact that, in the current context, monitoring alone cannot satisfy their legal obligations to prevent torture.

Indeed, the fact that the UN has documented abuses despite the existence of various ISAF countries' monitoring mechanisms and oversight by organizations like the Afghan Independent Human Rights Commission (AIHRC) speaks to the insufficiency of such measures. Given the sheer number of facilities and detainees, logistical and security challenges, and detainees' fears of reprisals for disclosing abuse, even the most well-designed monitoring mechanisms may in practice be incapable of ensuring detainees are free from torture.

There is a lack of professional capacity at every level of the Afghan justice system, from guards to judges to prosecutors.

An Urgent Need for Reform

International forces must also grapple with the problem of torture beyond the narrow issue of transfers, not least because they have been working so closely with the Afghan intelligence authorities, including using intelligence that may very well have been extracted through the use of torture. Appropriate assessment of the risk of torture will also always have to take into account treatment of *all* detainees at a particular Afghan facility—not just those transferred from international custody. Conceiving of the problem as one of detainee transfer also biases policy solutions towards bureaucratic box checking in order to resume detainee transfers—not actually halting abuse.

To be sure, there are real dilemmas and constraints facing the Afghan government and ISAF. There is a lack of professional capacity at every level of the Afghan justice system, from guards to judges to prosecutors. The sheer number of persons detained in connection with the conflict means the system is under severe strain, burdened further by the military as opposed to law enforcement nature of operations. But the Afghan government and all ISAF nations have strict legal obligations to refrain from and prevent torture, and as the UN report lays bare, they have fallen well short.

The looming troop drawdown and transition only give greater urgency to this issue. With more and more responsibility for security being shifted to Afghans, the strategic risk and political liability posed by abusive detention practices will only grow. Right now, the US and other ISAF nations have the most leverage to shape the Afghan justice system and leave behind institutions, laws, and mechanisms that uphold the rule of law and protect Afghans from torture. As the war in Afghanistan marks its tenth anniversary, time is not on the side of either ISAF or the Afghan government. The UN report marks a perhaps singular opportunity to marshal momentum behind detention reforms that will be long-lasting and effective at protecting the most basic of human rights.

VIEWPOINT 4

Youth in the United Kingdom Are Being Denied Due Process

Robert Stevens

In the following viewpoint, Robert Stevens argues that the basic tenets of the rule of law have been denied to those arrested during the rioting in Great Britain in August 2011. Stevens claims that a London Metropolitan Police Service document shows that authorities had a directive to keep all suspects from the rioting in custody without bail. He claims that such a policy, along with the ensuing harsh sentences, denies British youths their democratic rights. Stevens is a writer for the World Socialist Web Site.

As you read, consider the following questions:

1. According to Stevens, why did the Metropolitan Police Service believe it was impractical to offer bail to those arrested during the August 2011 rioting in London?
2. The author says that by August 22, 2011, police reportedly had arrested how many people in conjunction with the rioting?
3. What was the jail sentence for a Manchester man who took an ice cream cone during the looting, according to Stevens?

Robert Stevens, "Metropolitan Police Deny Due Process to British Youth," www.wsws.org, August 26, 2011.

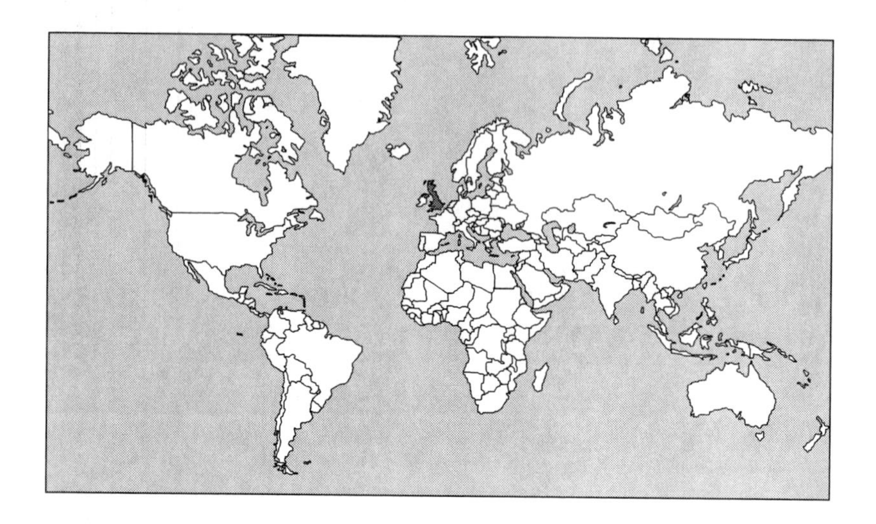

Three weeks after the outbreak of widespread rioting in London [which began August 6, 2011], the Metropolitan Police [Service, MPS, or the Met] continue to hunt down anyone suspected of involvement.

So far, the Metropolitan Police have arrested 2,006 people, including hundreds of juveniles. Of these, 1,135 people have been charged. The Met estimates that it will eventually arrest more than 3,000 people in London.

The Police Strategy

In carrying out this manhunt, the *Guardian* newspaper revealed this week that the Metropolitan Police have been operating what can only be described as an illegal "prisoner processing strategy". A document was circulated to every investigation officer as part of Operation Withern, set up by the Met, in response to the disturbances. . . .

The document proposed that no one arrested be allowed to be freed by giving them a caution, regardless of the offence. It also requests that everyone arrested be held in custody and recommends that bail should be denied when the case first goes to court.

"A strategic decision has been made by the MPS that, in all cases, an application will be made for remand in custody both at the police station, and later in court", it states.

The Met argues, "The volume of prisoners being processed makes it impractical to bail for the purpose of protracted investigation. Where evidence of an offence exists charging authority should be sought, that is likely to mean that the threshold test is applied."

The Metropolitan Police have been operating what can only be described as an illegal "prisoner processing strategy".

The test referred to allows prosecutors to lower the burden of proof needed to keep someone in custody only where there is reasonable suspicion and prospect of a conviction, and where there is a substantial risk to the public if they are released.

Against this, the Met has been charging suspects before collating all of the evidence required and before making basic necessary enquires. This is justified on the basis that the process of examining CCTV [closed-circuit television] footage and other enquires is not yet possible, "due to the ongoing public disorder in and around London".

An Unlawful Policy

The document became public after it was obtained by the solicitors Hodge, Jones & Allen, who are seeking a judicial review of the decisions of the police to refuse bail to one of their clients. They are defending a 25-year-old mother of two whom the Metropolitan Police decided not to bail after she was arrested with £2,500 worth of goods following the riots. There is no evidence that she was involved in any rioting or looting of shops.

Edward Kirton-Darling, a solicitor from Hodge, Jones & Allen, said he considered the policy outlined in the document to be unlawful. "The right to bail is a long-standing and essential part of our criminal justice system. It should be carefully considered and each case should be looked at on its own merits," he said.

He added, "In relation to the riots, it seems that the Metropolitan Police took a strategic decision to apply a blanket ban and deny everyone bail, no matter what their circumstances. I consider this policy is unlawful as a result."

In its letter to the Metropolitan Police, Kirton-Darling pointed out that such a policy was in breach of article 5 under the European Court of Human Rights, which guarantees an individual's liberty and security.

Hundreds, if not thousands, of people now face jail sentences as a result of this unprecedented dragnet.

Response by the Police

In response to the report in the *Guardian*, the Metropolitan Police issued a bald statement claiming that at "no point does the guidance issued to officers suggest that all persons arrested should be held in custody nor that cautions or other disposals are inappropriate in relation to Operation Withern."

Comments from the Met cited in the *Guardian* make clear that the issuing of such draconian guidance was bound up with "courts sitting extended hours" to process the hundreds of initial cases that were brought before them, following mass arrests during and following the riots. The Met said that "the recommendation that those charged were remanded in custody was made to ensure cases were dealt with quickly and again to protect the public from potential further disorder."

The Met statement attempted to deny that such a blanket policy was in existence by citing figures showing that by August 22 they had arrested a total of 1,881 people, of which 1,063 have been charged. According to the figures, 623 people have been bailed to return pending further inquiries. In what appears to be a clear indication that the "no caution" policy was in operation, the figures in fact reveal that just 17 people, out of 1,881, were cautioned.

Hundreds, if not thousands, of people now face jail sentences as a result of this unprecedented dragnet. All told, 1,406 suspects have now had an initial hearing at a magistrates' court. For those cases where the defendant is on remand, 62 percent were remanded in custody. Last year, just 10 percent of people brought before magistrates' courts were remanded in custody. As is the case nationally, many are being remanded by magistrates' courts, as they are only able to sentence people for up to six months in prison, or impose a £5,000 fine. If sent to crown court, a 10-year prison sentence can be handed down for offences such as burglary or riot.

Unprecedented attacks on democratic rights are being carried out.

This week, the first of those charged in London appeared at Wood Green Crown Court. One man was sentenced to 20 months in jail for violent disorder and another sentenced to six weeks' imprisonment for possessing an offensive weapon in Enfield during the riots.

The Harshest Sentences

The uncovering of the Met police guidance follows the disclosure last week that courts were imposing the harshest sentences on those charged with involvement in the riots, on the basis of a government directive. Novello Noades, chair of Camberwell Green Magistrates' Court in London, said before

The Government's Stance on Criminal Justice

On the radio last week [August 10, 2011] they interviewed one of the young men who'd been looting in Manchester.

He said he was going to carry on until he got caught.

This will be my first arrest, he said.

The prisons were already overflowing so he'd just get an ASBO [anti-social behaviour order], and he could live with that.

Well, we've got to show him and everyone like him that the party's over.

I know that when politicians talk about punishment and tough sentencing, people roll their eyes.

Yes, last week we saw the criminal justice system deal with an unprecedented challenge: The courts sat through the night and dispensed swift, firm justice.

We saw that the system was on the side of the law-abiding majority.

David Cameron, speech, August 15, 2011.

open court, "Our directive [from Her Majesty's Courts & Tribunals Service] for anyone involved in the rioting is a custodial sentence".

She later said she did not mean to use the term "directive".

Nationally, the most draconian sentences continue to be handed down for the pettiest of offences. On Thursday, 21-year-old Anderson Fernandes, who took an ice cream cone from a patisserie in Manchester after finding the door ajar during rioting on August 9, was jailed for 16 months. Another man, Jason Aitchison, 27, was sent down for four years, even though he had not stolen anything after a break-in at a jeweller—saying he did so "for a laugh".

Unprecedented attacks on democratic rights are being carried out. Children as young as 11 have been dragged before the courts and juveniles stripped of their right to anonymity. This week, a 12-year-old boy from Merseyside was arrested on "suspicion of violent disorder and criminal damage". A 16-year-old, Johnny Melfah from Worcestershire, was stripped of his anonymity this week after a court order was lifted.

Since 1933 and the introduction of an act of Parliament enforcing anonymity for juvenile offenders, only Melfah and three other children have ever been named.

The Response from the Prime Minister

On August 9, Prime Minister David Cameron spoke before a specially convened session of a recalled Parliament after initiating the national crackdown, via the government's emergency COBR [Cabinet Office Briefing Room] committee. In answer to a question by a Conservative MP [member of Parliament] whether the national football stadium should be used to detain those arrested en masse, Cameron said this would not be required, but told Parliament approvingly, "One police chief told me yesterday that it is time to tear up some of the manual on public order and restart it."

One day later, in authorising the use of water cannons in mainland Britain, Cameron said, "Whatever tactics the police feel they need to employ, they will have legal backing to do so".

The reality of this "legal backing" is the junking of democratic norms and the denial of the basic tenets of the rule of law to thousands of people in Britain, including hundreds of juveniles.

The London arrests are part of more than 3,000 already carried out nationally. In Birmingham, in the West Midlands, police have detained 523 people and charged 158 people with offences. Police in Merseyside have arrested more than 200 people. As of Monday, Greater Manchester Police (GMP) had arrested 295 people and charged 194. Forty-one cases have been heard in Manchester courts, with 32 people receiving a custodial sentence. The 32 jailed have been sentenced to an average of nearly 16 months in a prison or young offender institution.

VIEWPOINT 5

Russia Claws at the Rule of Law

Lynda Edwards

In the following viewpoint, Lynda Edwards argues that the Russian legal system is fraught with corruption and procedural defects. Edwards claims that lawyers face threats and even death for representing certain clients. Furthermore, she contends that the government has expanded law enforcement's ability to detain terrorism suspects prior to trial and has put a stamp of approval on torture. The recent murders of lawyers and journalists involved in high-profile cases, she concludes, leaves little hope for the restoration of the rule of law. Edwards was an award-winning writer for the ABA Journal *at the time this viewpoint was written.*

As you read, consider the following questions:

1. The author claims that what three harmful effects followed Russia's prosecution of Yukos Oil Company?
2. The airing of which three television shows is under attack by Russian prosecutors, according to Edwards?
3. Edwards claims that some Russians are hopeful for a restoration of the rule of law under what new president?

Lynda Edwards, "Russia Claws at the Rule of Law," *ABA Journal*, July 2009.

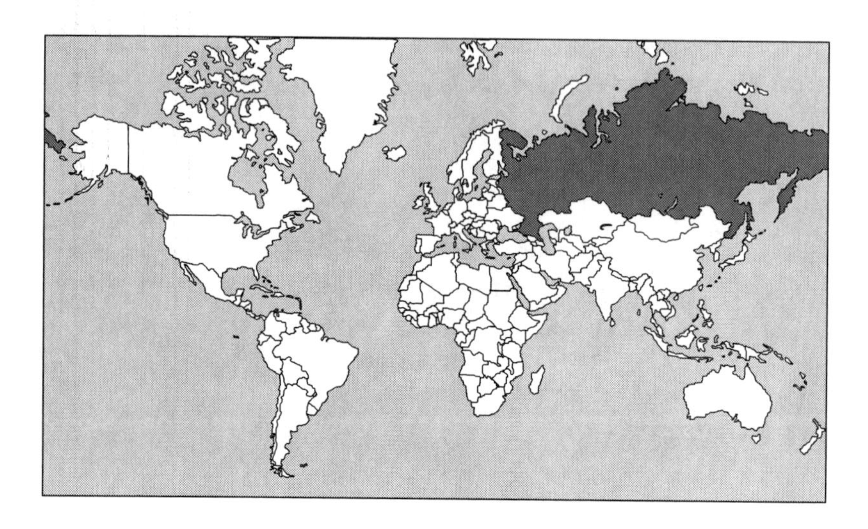

The courtroom gallery brimmed with lawyers during the trial in January of four men accused of murdering Anna Politkovskaya, a reporter for the Russian newspaper *Novaya Gazeta* who was gunned down in 2006 at the elevator of her Moscow apartment.

The newspaper had paid a high price for its investigations into political corruption. In 2000, another *Novaya* reporter had been beaten to death with hammers on a Moscow street. Three years later, the paper's managing editor died mysteriously from something that caused his skin to peel off.

For the lawyers gathered to watch it, the trial of those accused in Politkovskaya's murder was itself a victory. The very fact there was a trial at all signaled that the rule of law finally mattered in Russia.

Suddenly, cell phones began to chime across the courtroom with text messages; Politkovskaya's attorney—34-year-old human rights lawyer Stanislav Markelov—had been murdered. A young *Novaya Gazeta* intern walking with him was also shot and killed.

Markelov was founder and president of Russia's Rule of Law Institute. His murder had all the marks of a professional hit. He was shot point-blank in a crowd of people on a busy street by a gun topped with a silencer.

For lawyers in Russia these days, life is difficult, even dangerous.

To his colleagues, Markelov's killing came as no surprise. The only question was why. Was his assassination related to a Chechen murder, in which he was representing the victim's family? Or to the case of an environmentalist targeted by neo-Nazis? Or was it linked to attempts to stop the development of a mixed-use luxury real estate project?

Each matter involved powerful politicians, organized crime or well-connected military officers. And each seemed evidence to Markelov and his friends that the rule of law in 21st-century Russia is a captive of the rich, the powerful and the well connected.

For lawyers in Russia these days, life is difficult, even dangerous. Even attorneys who handle run-of-the-mill corporate work—including real estate deals, corporate contracts, environmental regulations and tax matters—have reported threats and harassment, according to the Moscow-based think tank Memorial Human Rights Center.

Though few will speak for attribution—or even allow their exact words to be quoted—American lawyers who once practiced in Russia say the law there has become increasingly politicized and unpredictable.

"A lawyer can keep a low profile and work on cases that never bring him close to peril, but the problem in Russia is, danger can lie in unexpected places," says Ethan Burger, an expert on Russia and an adjunct law professor at Georgetown University.

The Yukos Factor

A radical change in Russia's deference to due process can be traced to the government's enigmatic prosecution of Yukos Oil. U.S. investors lost an estimated $6 to $7 billion. Yukos executives lost their freedom. And lawyers who helped defend Yukos' interests are still feeling the reverberations.

From its beginning in the 1990s, Yukos was steeped in allegations of intrigue and violence. Created in 1993 after a controversial privatization of former Soviet assets, by 1999 Yukos was supplying 20 percent of Russia's oil production of 5.9 million barrels a day.

Handsome and charismatic, company founder and CEO Mikhail Khodorkovsky was once considered a potential rival to Vladimir Putin for the Russian presidency.

A radical change in Russia's deference to due process can be traced to the government's enigmatic prosecution of Yukos Oil.

In 2003, Khodorkovsky was arrested for fraud and, after months in prison, resigned from Yukos. Two years later he was convicted and sentenced to eight years in a Siberian prison. In March of this year, the Russian government began prosecuting Khodorkovsky on new charges of embezzlement and money laundering. He faces 22 more years in prison if convicted.

The U.S. State Department warned that the prosecution of Khodorkovsky had led to capital flight and a plunge in new foreign investment in Russia. Carol Patterson, a partner and nearly 20-year veteran of Baker & McKenzie's Moscow office, concedes that investing in Russia "requires thorough due diligence—both of the legal environment and of the people you are dealing with." But she believes the Khodorkovsky case is not representative of the business experience of most multinationals." Patterson notes that the "challenge in building corporate, tax and commercial law from scratch in 20 years has been immense," but "overall Russia has made tremendous progress."

By contrast, Robert Amsterdam—who represented Khodorkovsky until 2005, when Russian police burst into his hotel room and ordered him to leave the country—has little faith in Russia's legal system.

"Until the rule of law is established in Russia, I won't be back" says the Canadian attorney, who maintains an international practice based in London and Toronto that specializes in emerging markets. "I would advise lawyers to warn their clients not to invest in the raw materials in Russia. No timber, oil, mining, agriculture or fishing. There is too much political corruption in that sector."

John Pappalardo, a former U.S. attorney in Massachusetts who co-chairs Greenberg Traurig's white-collar practice group in Boston, became part of Khodorkovsky's defense team in 2003. A month before he arrived, Moscow police seized files belonging to Khodorkovsky's Russian lawyer, Anton Drel.

Pappalardo told the *Boston Globe* that the police had to remove a wall of Drel's office so they could cart off his mainframe computer. Pappalardo received a death threat by phone and said he never took cabs in Moscow for fear of being kidnapped.

Another Yukos attorney, Vasily Aleksanyan, was also imprisoned on charges of fraud. Aleksanyan, a Russian American who holds a master's in law from Harvard Law School, had headed the Yukos legal department since 1996 before he was appointed executive vice president in April 2006 and given a mandate to root out political corruption within the firm. Just days after his appointment, Aleksanyan was arrested for money laundering and fraud.

Aleksanyan's arrest became a human rights issue when it was revealed that he suffered from cancer, tuberculosis and AIDS while in prison, and had been refused proper medical attention. After international demands for his release, Aleksanyan, now 38, was freed in December after posting $1.8 million in bail.

In response to the Beslan attack, then president Putin demanded and received expanded powers of pretrial detention for terrorism suspects.

Chechen Terror

Another turning point—this in the law itself, rather than its application—came in the aftermath of the Beslan school massacre of 2004, which scarred the Russian psyche in much the same way Sept. 11 devastated Americans.

On the first day of school, 32 Chechen terrorists seized the Beslan elementary school, taking more than 1,100 parents, children and staff hostage.

After several hostages were murdered, Russian forces stormed the school with tanks and rockets. On TV sets across Russia, viewers saw the roof collapse on screaming victims as fire engulfed the school, leaving 334 hostages dead, 186 of them children.

In response to the Beslan attack, then president Putin demanded and received expanded powers of pretrial detention for terrorism suspects, including the use of "duress" in interrogations.

Christopher Osakwe, a retired Tulane University law professor now teaching at Moscow University, says the new powers are tough and broad. "Russian prosecutors are allowed unlimited pretrial detention without a charge," says Osakwe, who has provided the authoritative English translation of the Russian civil code.

"Russian judges and political rulers do not consider attorney-client confidentiality crucial to a proper defense. Russian officials can depose a defendant's attorney as a witness, making it impossible for him to continue representing his client," Osakwe says.

Osakwe's Moscow law students are often bewildered by the American debate over the legality of torture because "they find human rights are a somewhat alien concept," he says.

Russian lawyers don't have to be involved in human rights cases to suddenly find themselves on shaky legal ground. Last year, Russian prosecutors prepared a case against the nationwide 2x2 television network for broadcasting *The Simpsons, South Park* and *The Family Guy*. Prosecutors claim the cartoons violate Russian laws by "mocking patriotism, respect for family values and the importance of sport." As this magazine went to press, 2x2 was having trouble finding a lawyer to represent it.

Such cases can seem capricious and outright odd to an American ear. But lawyers who work in Russia say they have the very real effect of leaving legal boundaries so uncertain that even mundane transactions can involve personal risk to the lawyers involved.

An Inside Job

When he was arrested in November, Moscow tax lawyer Sergei Magnitsky was working for Firestone Duncan, a firm that offers legal, accounting and other financial services in Russia.

Magnitsky was charged with tax fraud for advice he gave in 2001 to Hermitage Capital Management, a British fund that invests in Russia, according to *BusinessWeek*. Jamison Firestone, managing partner of Moscow-based Firestone Duncan, has called the charges a fabrication, designed to pressure anyone associated with Hermitage Capital.

HSBC, the British bank that serves as trustee of Hermitage, filed a formal complaint with the Russian government about the apparent use of several Hermitage subsidiaries in a 2007 fraud. The companies were improperly reregistered under new owners and subsequently used to steal $230 million from the Russian treasury. The complaint implicates several members of Russia's interior ministry. After it was filed, in an apparent act of retaliation, three firms hired by Hermitage came under criminal investigation by Russian authorities.

According to the International Bar Association, Russian police raided the law offices of Eduard Khairetdinov last August. Khairetdinov, who was representing Hermitage Capital, was issued a summons, along with two other lawyers, demanding that the three appear as witnesses in a case they were involved in. "This not only contravenes Russian legislation, but also goes against the Basic Principles on the Role of Lawyers adopted by the United Nations," the IBA noted.

Fearing arrest, Khairetdinov and several other lawyers have since fled Russia.

Mark Ellis, executive director of the IBA, denounced the raids as a sign of deterioration of the rule of law in Russia. "When government agents interfere with the work of lawyers, it is not only the legal profession that is threatened, but the overall legal order in the state," said Ellis last September.

The Russian government has proposed a new law that would allow lawyers' licenses to be yanked without bar approval.

And in what critics say is an attempt to turn the legal profession against itself, the Russian government has been putting pressure on the lawyer-discipline process.

In the Yukos case, for instance, prosecutors tried to have all 14 attorneys who represented former CEO Khodorkovsky disbarred. The prosecutor-general singled out one attorney, human rights lawyer Karinna Moskalenko, for particular humiliation. He wanted her disbarred for "incompetent defense," even though Khodorkovsky wrote a statement praising her work.

Although disbarments would have curried favor with Putin, the Moscow collegium of advocates refused to disbar any of the attorneys. And perhaps as a result, the Russian government has proposed a new law that would allow lawyers' licenses to be yanked without bar approval.

A Hall of Mirrors

It is the hall of mirrors that is the murder of Stanislav Markelov which observers say best demonstrates the current troubled Russian legal landscape.

On the day he was killed, Markelov held a press conference about one of his cases—the rape, kidnapping and murder of an 18-year-old Chechen woman by Russian Col. Yuri Budanov.

Markelov represented the teenager's family during Budanov's trial. In 2003, Budanov was convicted of murder and sentenced to 10 years in prison, but he was released in January. Markelov announced at the press conference that he would challenge Budanov's release. Minutes later, Markelov was dead.

Markelov's friends are not sure whether it was the Budanov case that prompted his assassination. He also represented a number of Chechens who claimed to have been tortured or kidnapped by Russian officers and politicians, including the family of a Chechen student.

While preparing the case against a Russian police officer accused of falsely arresting, torturing and murdering the young man, Markelov was beaten by skinheads in a Moscow subway. They left his watch and wallet untouched, but stole his briefcase full of legal documents, says Markelov's friend and Russian human rights activist Oksana Chelysheva. Despite the intimidation, Markelov persisted, and the police officer was eventually sentenced to 11 years in jail.

Markelov's colleagues say his work representing newspaper editor Mikhail Beketov may be another case that led to his assassination. One of Beketov's stories probed Russian developers' plans to raze the ancient Khimki Forest near Moscow to build a luxury mixed-use real estate project.

Abusive phone callers began harassing Beketov at work and home. Someone poisoned Beketov's dog and left the corpse at the back door. In November, neighbors found Beketov unconscious and drenched in blood in his backyard. He was beaten so savagely, pieces of his shattered skull were pried from brain tissue. His mangled right leg and frostbitten fingers were amputated. The hospital received threatening phone calls vowing to "finish Beketov off."

Thanks to lobbying by Russian and American activists and lawyers, the comatose Beketov was moved to Sklifosovsky Scientific Research Institute, Russia's leading emergency care center.

Crimes such as Markelov's murder are handled by the 50,000-lawyer Procuracy—the entity that investigates and prosecutes crimes. It is considered the elite of the legal profession, and has been credited with jailing Russian street criminals and taking back financial institutions from mob control.

But in a paper coauthored with New York University School of Law professor Mary Holland, Burger says the agency "has been otherwise ineffective when it comes to cases treading on government interests and those of high-level officials."

"The Procuracy reflects the interests of the presidential administration and the elites within it," explains Burger. "It has not solved any of the politically motivated contract murders in recent years."

Moscow's Answer

Asked for its views on the state of the rule of law, the Russian Embassy's press office deferred to former presidential adviser Andranik Migranyan of Russia's Institute for Democracy and Cooperation.

"The 1990s were wild times, people grabbing all they could during a period of privatization with a weakened central government and weak law enforcement. People were not placing faith in the judicial system, just settling scores and feuds themselves," says Migranyan.

"Things are much better, much calmer now. There is a strong government. Our current president, Dmitry Anatolyevich Medvedev, is a lawyer himself," Migranyan notes.

Prosecutors, he says, need to learn how to be competitive in the courtroom. "Medvedev said the days when prosecutors could rely on presumption of guilt are over. Guilt must be proved."

Medvedev himself stirred hopes among lawyers in a January 2008 speech. "Russia is a country of legal nihilism. No European country can boast such a universal disregard for the rule of law," said Medvedev. "Corruption in the official structures has a huge scale and the fight against it should become a national program."

Markelov's friends are not holding their breath for the start of a government campaign in support of the rule of law.

Meanwhile, police have no suspects and no leads in the assassination of Markelov and Baburova. However, they did show up to see the two buried.

Markelov's friends are not holding their breath for the start of a government campaign in support of the rule of law.

At Markelov's funeral, each mourner at the graveside tossed a handful of dirt on the coffin. *Novaya Gazeta* reported that the crowd was so big "the gravediggers had very little work to do in the end." And on the day the newspaper buried its former lawyer, its front-page headline read, "We Are Not Afraid."

VIEWPOINT 6

In Several Countries in Asia, Unfair Trials Are Too Common

Anti-Death Penalty Asia Network (ADPAN)

In the following viewpoint, the Anti-Death Penalty Asia Network (ADPAN) argues that multiple failures of due process deny suspects a fair trial in the Asia-Pacific region, and this is of particular concern with death penalty cases. ADPAN claims that despite international law to the contrary, countries continue to deny suspects their due process rights in custody and impose mandatory death sentences for minor offenses. ADPAN is a network of non-governmental organizations (NGOs), civil society groups, lawyers, and individual members working for the abolition of the death penalty across Asia and the Pacific.

As you read, consider the following questions:

1. According to the author, how many capital offenses are there in China, Pakistan, Taiwan, and Vietnam?
2. Which countries impose a mandatory death sentence for mere possession of drugs over a certain amount, according to the author?
3. According to the author, what system in Japan denies suspects adequate access to legal counsel?

Anti-Death Penalty Asia Network (ADPAN), "Lethal Injustice in Asia: End Unfair Trials, Stop Executions," December 2011. www.adpan.net. AI Index: ASA 01/022/2011

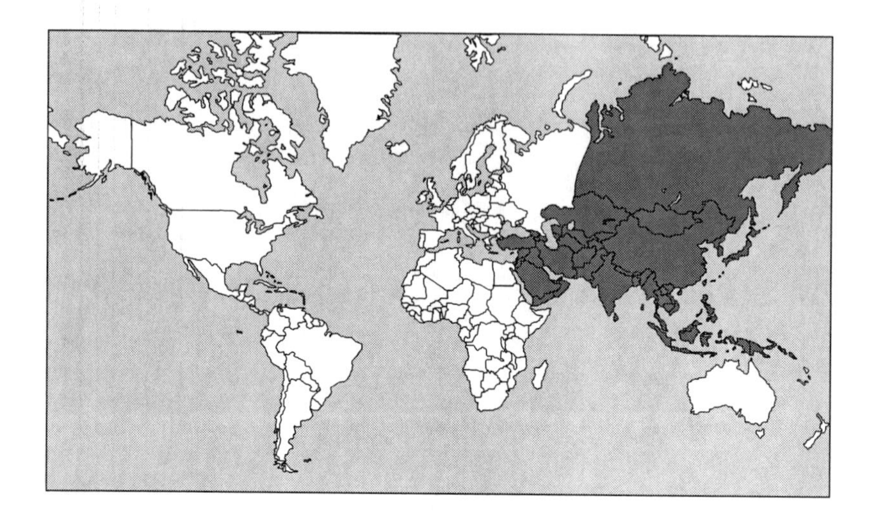

The basic principles of the right to a fair trial are reflected in law throughout the world and set out in the 1948 Universal Declaration of Human Rights (UDHR), the cornerstone of human rights law. These principles were elaborated in 1966 in article 14 of the International Covenant on Civil and Political Rights (ICCPR). . . . The right to a fair trial has become legally binding on all states as part of customary international law, whether or not they have ratified relevant treaties. Of those countries that retain and use the death penalty in the Asia-Pacific region, only Malaysia, Myanmar [also known as Burma] and Singapore have not signed or ratified the ICCPR.

The Right to a Fair Trial in Death Penalty Cases

In cases where the life of the accused is at stake, it is all the more important that fair trial principles are rigorously applied. In 1984, the UN [United Nations] Economic and Social Council (ECOSOC) introduced safeguards to further protect the right to a fair trial for those facing the death penalty. These are based on the premise that in death penalty cases, safeguards should go "above and beyond" the normal protections given to people facing criminal charges. This is because death penalty cases involve the right to life, and the arbitrary deprivation of life is prohibited under article 6 (right to life) of the ICCPR. Sentencing someone to death following a trial that does not respect basic fair trial standards violates the right to life of that person.

Despite UN guidelines specifying that the death penalty can only be imposed for intentional crimes with lethal consequences, people in the Asia-Pacific region are executed for crimes ranging from drug trafficking to theft.

There are at least 55 capital offences in China, 28 in Pakistan, 57 in Taiwan and 21 in Vietnam. In North Korea, a number of political offences are punishable with death including "conspiracy to overturn the state" and "treason against the fatherland". In some countries, the death penalty is imposed for actions which, under international law, should not be treated as a criminal offence at all. In Pakistan, blasphemy carries the death penalty, although no one is known to have been executed on these grounds. In Afghanistan, people have been sentenced to death for converting from Islam to another religion, even though "apostasy" is not included as an offence in Afghanistan's penal code.

In cases where the life of the accused is at stake, it is all the more important that fair trial principles are rigorously applied.

Challenges to the Right to a Fair Trial

In many countries in the region, the right to a fair trial is impeded by laws which deny due process. Even in countries where due process safeguards exist in principle, they often do not apply in practice.

Courts continue to rely on confessions extracted through torture as evidence in criminal trials—despite the international ban on torture. They impose mandatory death sentences for crimes such as drug trafficking. They place the burden of proof on the accused, depriving them of the right to be presumed innocent. Access to a lawyer before, during and after trial is regularly denied, and in some countries the independence of the judiciary is far from assured. And in times of alleged security or political crises, states often resort to special courts, condemning people to death after hasty proceedings.

Once the accused has been sentenced to death, he or she has the right under international law to appeal to a higher court against the sentence and to seek clemency or commutation of that sentence. But in some countries, neither of these avenues are available.

Government officials in many Asia-Pacific states argue that the enforcement of criminal justice falls exclusively within the authority of each state, but the conduct of trials is subject to international law and standards. These laws and standards are never more important than in circumstances where the state uses its power to take the irreversible step of depriving someone of his or her life.

The Existence of Torture and Other Cruel Treatment

The ban on torture and other cruel, inhuman or degrading treatment is absolute in international law. International fair trial standards are explicit that no one should be forced to testify against themselves or to confess guilt. The UN Convention Against Torture and Other Cruel, Inhuman or Degrading Treatment or Punishment (Convention Against Torture) states that information extracted through torture must not be used as evidence in court. Yet most countries in the region that retain the death penalty tolerate torture or other ill-treatment as a means of inducing confessions, even though their own laws forbid its use. Courts regularly ignore evidence of torture and other ill-treatment when sentencing people to death.

China ratified the Convention Against Torture in 1988, and Chinese law prohibits the use of torture to extort confessions. The authorities have also passed a number of regulations in recent years aimed at strengthening this prohibition and reinforcing procedures to tackle the use of other illegally obtained evidence, especially in death penalty cases. Nevertheless, Chinese law still fails to include an explicit ban on the use of all evidence extracted through torture and ill-treatment in court cases. People continue to be executed despite strong evidence that their conviction was based on confessions extracted through torture.

Indonesia's constitution prohibits the use of torture. The Indonesian criminal code states that any information a suspect provides to police must be free from coercion, but Indonesia has yet to make torture a criminal offence. Similarly, the law in a number of other countries including Afghanistan and India contains specific protections against coerced confessions. Yet torture by police is widespread in these countries, and forced confessions are regularly relied upon as evidence during trials. In Japan and Taiwan, heavy and sometimes sole reliance is placed on confessions.

The ban on torture and other cruel, inhuman or degrading treatment is absolute in international law.

The Imposition of Mandatory Death Sentences

Mandatory death sentences prevent judges from exercising their discretion and from considering all factors in a case. Mandatory death sentences are prohibited under international law as they have been found to constitute arbitrary deprivation of life and cruel, inhuman or degrading punishment. Many courts and judicial bodies have ruled them unconstitutional.

In 2010, the Supreme Court of Bangladesh ruled the mandatory death sentences for murder after rape as unconstitutional. The Indian Supreme Court has ruled such sentences for murder unconstitutional, and in June 2011 the Bombay High Court ruled that mandatory death sentences for repeat offences under the Narcotic Drug and Psychotropic Substances Act violated the right to life. In 2006, the mandatory death penalty was removed from two laws in Taiwan.

A number of countries continue to impose mandatory death sentences, particularly for drug offences. Brunei, Laos, Malaysia, North Korea, Pakistan and Singapore all impose such sentences for possession of drugs over a certain amount regardless of whether the person was in possession of a relatively small quantity or was dealing in substantial amounts. Imposing the death penalty for drug offences breaches international law which permits the death penalty only for the "most serious crimes".

Mandatory death sentences are prohibited under international law as they have been found to constitute arbitrary deprivation of life and cruel, inhuman or degrading punishment.

The Principle of Presumed Innocence

A core principle of international law is that anyone charged with a criminal offence must be presumed innocent until and unless proved guilty according to law in a fair trial. The right to be presumed innocent applies not only at trial but before trial as well. It applies to suspects before criminal charges are filed and carries through until a conviction is confirmed following a final appeal. The ECOSOC safeguards elaborate on this right, stressing that the death penalty may be imposed only when "the guilt of the person charged is based upon clear and convincing evidence leaving no room for an alternative explanation of the facts."

Countries with Laws That Provide for Mandatory Death Sentences, Including for Drug Offenses and Other Nonviolent Crimes

TAKEN FROM: Anti-Death Penalty Asia Network (ADPAN), "Lethal Injustice in Asia: End Unfair Trials, Stop Executions," December 2011.

However, the laws in a number of Asia-Pacific countries violate this right, providing in effect for a reversal of the burden of proof in the case of certain crimes. Defendants charged with such crimes in those countries are presumed guilty and bear the onus of proving their innocence.

In China, the principle of presumption of innocence is entirely absent from the Criminal Procedure Law. In Taiwan, the law was only recently changed to include the presumption of innocence. Those found to be knowingly carrying drugs over a certain quantity in Malaysia and Singapore are presumed to be guilty of trafficking, for which there is a mandatory sentence of death.

The Right to Legal Counsel

Access to a lawyer from the outset of detention is a key safeguard against torture and other ill-treatment, and vital to ensuring a fair trial. The right to a fair trial requires that the accused has access to a lawyer not only during the trial itself, but also immediately on arrest, during detention, interrogation and preliminary investigations. The right to a lawyer generally means that a person has the right to legal counsel of their choice. If defendants do not have their own lawyers, they are entitled to have lawyers assigned by a judge or judicial authority. If the defendant cannot afford to pay, assigned counsel must be provided free of charge, and in death penalty cases, should reflect the choice of the accused.

Access to a lawyer from the outset of detention is a key safeguard against torture and other ill-treatment, and vital to ensuring a fair trial.

The right to counsel means the right to competent counsel. The [UN] Human Rights Committee has stated that counsel for those facing the death penalty must be "effective in the representation of the accused" at all stages of the trial. It has also said that if they show "blatant misbehaviour or incompetence" the state may be responsible for a violation of the right to fair trial.

The right to be defended by counsel includes the right to confidential communications with counsel and to adequate time and facilities to prepare the defence. In death penalty cases, the accused should be given time and facilities to prepare their defence that goes above and beyond that given for other cases. This includes providing free translation and interpretation services where needed. The accused and their counsel should have opportunities equal to that of the prosecution to present their case. If the authorities hinder lawyers from fulfilling their task effectively, the state may be held responsible for violating the right to a fair trial.

The Right to a Fair Trial

Across the region, prisoners facing the death penalty have little or no access to lawyers following arrest and when preparing for trial or appeal processes.

In China, authorities may block or make it very difficult for defence lawyers to meet with their clients, gather evidence and access case documents. Lawyers defending clients involved in politically sensitive cases have been intimidated. Others have had charges filed against them for advising their clients to withdraw forced confessions or for trying to introduce evidence that challenges the prosecution's case.

In Japan, the *daiyo kangoku* system allows the police to detain and interrogate suspects for up to 23 days. The detainee has no access to a lawyer during interrogation on the assumption that a lawyer's presence would make it harder for police to "persuade the suspect to tell the truth". . . .

Every person charged with an offence has the right to a fair trial. When defendants are denied due process in criminal trials they are denied justice.

In the Asia-Pacific region, thousands of people are being sentenced to death and executed every year after unfair trials which fail to comply with international standards, undermining the rule of law and violating the right to life, the right to a fair trial and the ban on torture and other ill-treatment.

Periodical and Internet Sources Bibliography

The following articles have been selected to supplement the diverse views presented in this chapter.

Elliott Abrams	"Due Process in Bahrain?," *Pressure Points*, October 6, 2011. http://blogs.cfr.org.
Sarah Boseley	"Fears of Rough Justice as Courts Rush to Process Riot Arrests," *Guardian* (UK), August 11, 2011.
Marjorie Cohn	"Obama's Guantánamo Appeasement Plan," Common Dreams, May 26, 2009. www.commondreams.org.
Mark Engler	"Guantanamo Has Got to Go: Protesting Ten Years of Indefinite Detention," *Dissent*, January 12, 2012.
Financial Times	"Erdogan, Justice and the Rule of Law," January 10, 2012.
Stephen Lendman	"ICRC's Damning Expose of US Torture," *SteveLendmanBlog*, April 13, 2009. http://sjlendman.blogspot.com
Andrew C. McCarthy	"Due Process for Jihadists?," *Weekly Standard*, December 17, 2007.
Feisal G. Mohamed	"A Farewell to Due Process: The Assassination of Anwar al-Awlaki," *Dissent*, October 3, 2011.
Tom Parker	"10 Years On, 10 Reasons Guantanamo Must Be Closed," *Human Rights Now*, January 11, 2012. http://blog.amnestyusa.org.
Peter Tatchell	"One Year in Jail, Bradley Manning Is a Hero," *New Statesman*, May 18, 2011.

Chapter 4

The Right to Privacy

VIEWPOINT 1

Worldwide, Diverse Rules and Opinions Exist Concerning Online Privacy

Economist

In the following viewpoint, the Economist *argues that data protection regulations around the world vary widely. The author claims that Europe's new privacy directive is stricter than American standards of privacy, posing a conundrum for companies that have a presence in both places. Additionally, the author contends that privacy legislation likely to come out of China and India will be very different than restrictions seen in the European Union and the United States, further complicating the development of a uniform data protection procedure. The* Economist *is a global newspaper of analysis and opinion.*

As you read, consider the following questions:

1. According to the author, the European Union's justice commissioner claims that its new privacy regulation will save businesses how much money per year?
2. What percentage of Europeans do not trust Internet companies to protect their personal information, according to the author?
3. According to the author, are the future privacy regulations of China and India likely to be more stringent or less stringent than those of the European Union?

"Private Data, Public Rules," *The Economist*, January 28, 2012. Reproduced by permission.

First came the yodelling, then the pain. The online entrepreneurs and venture capitalists at DLD [Digital Life Design conference], a geeks' shindig this month [January 2012] in Munich, barely had time to recover from their traditional Bavarian entertainment before Viviane Reding, the European Union's [EU's] justice commissioner, introduced a new privacy regulation. Ms Reding termed personal data the "currency" of the digital economy. "And like any currency it needs stability and trust," Ms Reding told the assembled digerati.

Europe's New Privacy Regulation

The EU's effort (formally published on January 25th) is part of a global government crackdown on the commercial use of personal information.

A White House report, out soon, is expected to advocate a consumer privacy law. China has issued several draft guidelines on the issue and India has a privacy bill in the works. But their approaches differ dramatically. As data whizz across borders, creating workable rules for business out of varying national standards will be hard.

Europe's new privacy regulation is one of the most sweeping. Its first goal is to build a "digital single market". That will be a welcome change from the patchwork of rules that has grown up since the previous privacy directive in 1995. When Google's Street View mapping service accidentally captured personal data from some open, unsecured Wi-Fi networks in the houses it photographed, some EU countries told the firm to delete the data. Others told it to hold the information indefinitely.

The commission hopes that when the new regulation comes into effect (probably in 2016) it will clear up this mess. A firm based in, say, Ireland will be able to obey Irish law and do business across the EU, without worrying whether it is in line with other countries' rules. A new European Data Protection Board will enforce the regime. And if a company faces judicial proceedings in two member states, the courts will be obliged to communicate. Ms Reding expects these changes to save business €2.3 billion ($3 billion) a year.

As data whizz across borders, creating workable rules for business out of varying national standards will be hard.

Challenges of the Directive

But the new regime is tougher as well as being uniform. Firms must gain proper consent (defined strictly) before using and processing data. They may collect no more information than is necessary and keep it only while they need it. Children's data gain extra safeguards. Users must be able to move information from one service provider to another (for example, an address book between two social networks).

The EU's 500m [million] residents will also win a brand new right: to be forgotten. Users can not only request that a company show what data it holds on them; they can also demand that it deletes all copies. Critics say this is impractical, vague, and overambitious. It is hard to say where one man's data end and another's begin. And once something is online, it is virtually impossible to ensure that all copies are deleted. Small firms will struggle; even big ones will find the planned penalties steep.

Even more contentiously, the directive covers any firm that does business with Europeans, even if it is based outside the EU. America's Department of Commerce sent the commission a strong 15-page protest, saying that the directive "could hinder commercial interoperability while unintentionally diminishing consumer privacy protection".

American and European Opinion on Privacy

That stance reflects differences in American and European attitudes towards data protection, and indeed to regulation in general. America has avoided overly prescriptive privacy legislation, believing that companies should generally regulate themselves. Only when firms fail at self-regulation does the Federal Trade Commission (FTC) step in. It has broad powers to tackle unfair and deceptive practices, and has not hesitated to use them. In recent rulings, Google and Facebook agreed to a biennial audit of their privacy policies and practices for the next 20 years.

For the global digital economy, differences in privacy laws are a kind of trade barrier and a costly brake on innovation.

European sensitivities are different. A Eurobarometer poll last year found that 62% of Europeans do not trust Internet companies to protect their personal information. A big reason is history. In the 1930s, Dutch officials compiled an impressive national registry. This later enabled the Nazis to identify 73% of Dutch Jews, compared with just 25% in less efficient France, notes Viktor Mayer-Schönberger of Oxford University in his book *Delete: The Virtue of Forgetting in the Digital Age.*

For the global digital economy, differences in privacy laws are a kind of trade barrier and a costly brake on innovation. In the past, Europe and America reached a compromise with the "safe harbour" framework of 2000. As long as American companies adhered to certain principles based on the 1995 directive, they could do business in the EU.

Privacy Regulation in America

The arrangement has worked well, but America now worries that when its new rules come in the EU may want to rejig the deal. America might have more bargaining power if it had its own privacy law on the statute books, some experts argue; in any case, public concern about data protection is growing there. On January 24th Google triggered an outcry when it

European Opinion on the Right to Be Forgotten

In what circumstances, if any, would you like personal information stored and collected through a website to be completely deleted?

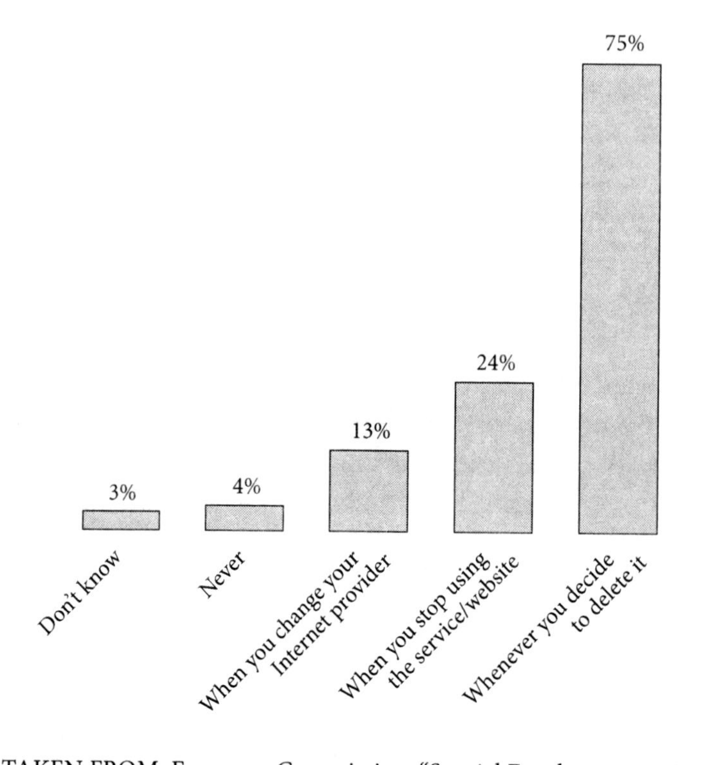

TAKEN FROM: European Commission, "Special Eurobarometer 359: Attitudes on Data Protection and Electronic Identity in the European Union," June 2011.

announced that from March it will share data gleaned from people logged into any of its services with all of its businesses, whether those users like it or not.

The administration is hurrying to catch up. In its report, the White House will recommend a legal framework for privacy, plus new codes of conduct. The chances of legislation passing in an election year are slim, even on what is usually a bipartisan issue. Talks among business lobbies, privacy activists and regulators may at least produce non-statutory codes, though without the imminent threat of legislation some companies may dawdle.

The FTC will also release a privacy report later this year. This will look broadly at the use of personal data being scooped up by companies on- and off-line. Among other things, it is likely to applaud progress in letting Internet users take steps to block tracking by tweaking their web browsers. It will probably support a tougher regime for brokers of consumer data and an industry initiative to give web pages special icons that people can use to prevent firms from tracking their activity.

America and Europe will set the global standards. But other countries' privacy rules matter too.

China's and India's Proposed Privacy Laws

America and Europe will set the global standards. But other countries' privacy rules matter too. China and India will soon have more people online than Europe and America have citizens. Neither Asian country has yet passed formal national legislation, but both are considering it—with every indication that their new laws will outdo even Europe in their severity.

India's draft privacy bill will set up a data-protection authority, call for consent before personal data can be processed and create a formal "right to privacy". Critics say the bill is too broad and that clauses protecting an individual's "honour and good name" could be used for censorship.

China's draft personal information protection law was proposed in 2003, but has since languished, leading to both regional experimentation and some big ad hoc rulings from ministries. The resulting hotchpotch leaves businesses and consumers confused. But in January 2011 the Ministry of Industry and Information Technology issued draft rules on data protection that restrict the ability of organisations to transfer personal data without specific prior informed consent.

These define personal information broadly, as anything that can identify an individual either on its own or in combination with other data. They also appear to forbid the export of personal information—even, on one reading, from one division of a company to another. That could hamper multinationals which need to send data across national borders. And it could hit outsourcers trying to deal with their customers. A further danger is that China's regulations are often arbitrarily or selectively enforced. Some information-processing firms are said to have moved their operations to Hong Kong, which has laxer and more predictable rules.

Building a single European data-protection regime is hard enough. Harmonising it smoothly with America will be harder. Reaching deals with Indian bureaucrats and Chinese mandarins set to defend the interests and the data of their countries' rapidly growing online firms may be downright impossible. Welcome to the new world of data geopolitics.

VIEWPOINT 2

The Right to Be Forgotten

Jeffrey Rosen

In the following viewpoint, Jeffrey Rosen argues that the "right to be forgotten," established by the European Union's new data protection regulation threatens freedom of expression. Rosen argues that although it is uncontroversial for people to have the right to delete material on the Internet that they have posted about themselves, it is a threat to free speech to establish a right to have individuals remove information that others have posted about them, whether it is true or not. Rosen is a professor of law at George Washington University and the Legal Affairs Editor of the New Republic.

As you read, consider the following questions:

1. Rosen claims that intellectual roots of the European right to be forgotten can be found in what law?
2. What is the second category of takedown requests that the author identifies as being affected by the new European privacy regulation?
3. What is the third category of takedown requests that the author identifies as being affected by the new European privacy regulation?

Jeffrey Rosen, "The Right to Be Forgotten," *Stanford Law Review*, vol. 64, February 13, 2012, pp. 88–92. Symposium Issue: The Privacy Paradox: Privacy and Its Conflicting Values. Reproduced by permission.

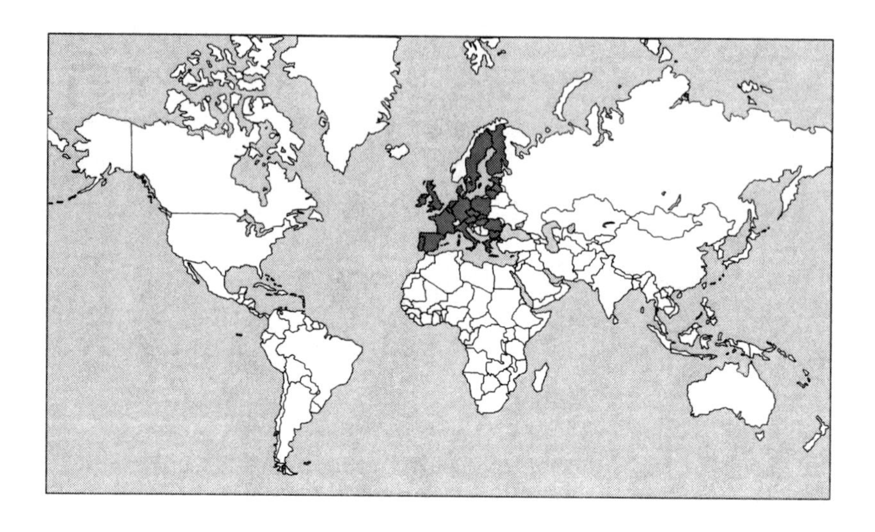

At the end of January, the European Commissioner for Justice, Fundamental Rights and Citizenship, Viviane Reding, announced the European Commission's proposal to create a sweeping new privacy right—the "right to be forgotten." The right, which has been hotly debated in Europe for the past few years, has finally been codified as part of a broad new proposed data protection regulation. Although Reding depicted the new right as a modest expansion of existing data privacy rights, in fact it represents the biggest threat to free speech on the Internet in the coming decade. The right to be forgotten could make Facebook and Google, for example, liable for up to two percent of their global income if they fail to remove photos that people post about themselves and later regret, even if the photos have been widely distributed already. Unless the right is defined more precisely when it is promulgated over the next year or so, it could precipitate a dramatic clash between European and American conceptions of the proper balance between privacy and free speech, leading to a far less open Internet.

In theory, the right to be forgotten addresses an urgent problem in the digital age: It is very hard to escape your past on the Internet now that every photo, status update, and tweet lives forever in the cloud. But Europeans and Americans have diametrically opposed approaches to the problem. In Europe, the intellectual roots of the right to be forgotten can be found in French law, which recognizes *le droit à l'oubli*—or the "right of oblivion"—a right that allows a convicted criminal who has served his time and been rehabilitated to object to the publication of the facts of his conviction and incarceration. In America, by contrast, publication of someone's criminal history is protected by the First Amendment, leading Wikipedia to resist the efforts by two Germans convicted of murdering a famous actor to remove their criminal history from the actor's Wikipedia page.[1]

European regulators believe that all citizens face the difficulty of escaping their past now that the Internet records everything and forgets nothing—a difficulty that used to be limited to convicted criminals. When Commissioner Reding announced the new right to be forgotten on January 22, she noted the particular risk to teenagers who might reveal compromising information that they would later come to regret. She then articulated the core provision of the "right to be forgotten": "If an individual no longer wants his personal data to be processed or stored by a data controller, and if there is no legitimate reason for keeping it, the data should be removed from their system."[2]

In endorsing the new right, Reding downplayed its effect on free speech. "It is clear that the right to be forgotten cannot amount to a right of the total erasure of history," she said.[3] And relying on Reding's speeches, press accounts of the newly proposed right to be forgotten have been similarly reassuring about its effect on free speech. In a post at the Atlantic .com, "Why Journalists Shouldn't Fear Europe's 'Right to be

1. John Schwartz, *Two German Killers Demanding Anonymity Sue Wikipedia's Parent*, N.Y. Times, Nov. 12, 2009, at A13; *see alsoWalter Sedlmayr*, Wikipedia (last visited Feb. 6, 2012), http://en.wikipedia.org/wiki/Walter_Sedlmayr.
2. Viviane Reding, Vice President, Eur. Comm'n, The EU Data Protection Reform 2012: Making Europe the Standard Setter for Modern Data Protection Rules in the Digital Age 5 (Jan. 22, 2012), *available at* http://europa.eu/rapid/pressReleasesAction.do ?reference=SPEECH/12/26&format=PDF.
3. *Id.*

Forgotten,'" John Hendel writes that although the original proposals a year ago "would have potentially given people the ability to cull any digital reference—from the public record, journalism, or social networks—they deemed irrelevant and unflattering," Reding had proposed a narrower definition of data that people have the right to remove: namely "personal data [people] have given out themselves."[4] According to Hendel "[t]his provision is key. The overhaul insists that Internet users control the data *they* put online, not the references in media or anywhere else."[5]

But Hendel seems not to have parsed the regulations that were actually proposed three days later on January 25. They are not limited to personal data that people "have given out themselves"; instead, they create a new right to delete personal data, defined broadly as "any information relating to a data subject."[6] For this reason, they arguably create a legally enforceable right to demand the deletion of any photos or data that I post myself, even after they've gone viral, not to mention unflattering photos that include me or information about me that others post, whether or not it is true.

In a widely cited blog post last March, Peter Fleischer, chief privacy counsel of Google, notes that the right to be forgotten, as discussed in Europe, often covers three separate categories, each of which proposes progressively greater threats to free speech.[7] And the right to be forgotten, as proposed at the end of January, arguably applies in all three of Fleischer's categories.

4. John Hendel, *Why Journalists Shouldn't Fear Europe's 'Right to Be Forgotten,'* Atlantic (Jan. 25, 2012), http://www.theatlantic.com/technology/archive/2012/01/why-journalists-shouldnt-fear-europes-right-to-be-forgotten/251955/.

5. *Id.*

6. *Commission Proposal for a Regulation of the European Parliament and of the Council,* art. 4(2), COM (2012) 11 final (Jan. 25, 2012) , *available at* http://ec.europa.eu/justice/data-protection/document/review2012/com_2012_11_en.pdf.

7. Peter Fleischer, *Foggy Thinking About the Right to Oblivion,* Privacy . . . ? (Mar. 9, 2011), http://peterfleischer.blogspot.com/2011/03/foggy-thinking-about-right-to-oblivion.html.

The first category is the least controversial: "If I post something online, do I have the right to delete it again?" This involves cases where I post a photo on Facebook and later think better of it and want to take it down. Since Facebook and other social networking sites already allow me to do this, creating a legally enforceable right here is mostly symbolic and entirely unobjectionable. As proposed, the European right to be forgotten would also usefully put pressure on Facebook to abide by its own stated privacy policies by allowing users to confirm that photos and other data have been deleted from its archives after they are removed from public display.

But the right to delete data becomes far more controversial when it involves Fleischer's second category: "If I post something, and someone else copies it and re-posts it on their own site, do I have the right to delete it?" Imagine a teenager regrets posting a picture of herself with a bottle of beer on her own site and after deleting it, later discovers that several of her friends have copied and re-posted the picture on their own sites. If she asks them to take down the pictures, and her friends refuse or cannot be found, should Facebook be forced to delete the picture from her friends' albums without the owners' consent based solely on the teenager's objection?

According to the proposed European right to forget, the default answer is almost certainly yes. According to the regulation, when someone demands the erasure of personal data, an Internet service provider "shall carry out the erasure without delay," unless the retention of the data is "necessary" for exercising "the right of freedom of expression," as defined by member states in their local laws.[8] In another section, the regulation creates an exemption from the duty to remove data for "the processing of personal data solely for journalistic purposes, or for the purposes of artistic or literary expression."[9] Essentially, this puts the burden on Facebook to prove to a

8. Proposed Data Protection Regulation, *supra* note 6, at art. 17(3).
9. *Id.* at art. 80.

The European Commission's Explanation of the Right to Be Forgotten

I want to explicitly clarify that people shall have the right—and not only the 'possibility'—to withdraw their consent to the processing of the personal data they have given out themselves.

The Internet has an almost unlimited search and memory capacity. So even tiny scraps of personal information can have a huge impact, even years after they were shared or made public. The right to be forgotten will build on already existing rules to better cope with privacy risks online. It is the individual who should be in the best position to protect the privacy of their data by choosing whether or not to provide it. It is therefore important to empower [European Union] citizens, particularly teenagers, to be in control of their own identity online.

Viviane Reding,
"The EU Data Protection Reform 2012:
Making Europe the Standard Setter for Modern
Data Protection Rules in the Digital Age,"
speech at the Digital Life Design conference in Munich,
Germany, January 24, 2012.

European Commission authority that my friend's publication of my embarrassing picture is a legitimate journalistic (or literary or artistic) exercise. If I contact Facebook, where I originally posted the embarrassing picture, it must take "all reasonable steps" on its own to identify any relevant third parties and secure the takedown of the content.[10] At the very least, Facebook will have to engage in the kinds of difficult line-drawing exercises previously performed by courts. And the

10. *Id.* at art. 17(2).

prospect of ruinous monetary sanctions for any data controller that "does not comply with the right to be forgotten or to erasure"—a fine up to 1,000,000 euros or up to two percent of Facebook's annual worldwide income[11]—could lead data controllers to opt for deletion in ambiguous cases, producing a serious chilling effect.

For a preview of just how chilling that effect might be, consider the fact that the right to be forgotten can be asserted not only against the publisher of content (such as Facebook or a newspaper) but against search engines like Google and Yahoo that link to the content. The Spanish data protection authority, for example, has sued Google to force it to delete links to embarrassing newspaper articles that are legal under Spanish law.[12] And suits against third-party intermediaries are also threatening freedom of speech in Argentina, as the case of Virginia Da Cunha shows. The Argentine pop star had posed for racy pictures when she was young, but recently sued Google and Yahoo to take them down, arguing that they violated the Argentine version of the "right to be forgotten." Google replied that it could not comply technologically with a broad legal injunction demanding the removal of the pictures, and Yahoo said that the only way to comply would be to block all sites referring to Da Cunha for its Yahoo search engines. Nevertheless, an Argentine judge sided with Da Cunha and after fining Google and Yahoo, ordered them to remove all sites containing sexual images that contained her name. The decision was overturned on appeal, on the grounds that Google and Yahoo could only be held liable if they knew content was defamatory and negligently failed to remove it. But there are at least one hundred and thirty similar cases pending in Argentine courts demanding removal of photos and user-generated content, mostly brought by entertainers and mod-

11. *Id.* at art. 79(5)(c), (6)(c).
12. Peter Fleischer, *The Right to Be Forgotten, or How to Edit Your History*, Privacy . . . ? (Jan. 29, 2012), http://peterfleischer.blogspot.com/2012/01/right-to-be-forgotten-or-how-to-edit.html.

els. The plaintiffs include the *Sports Illustrated* swimsuit model Yesica Toscanini; when a user of Yahoo Argentina plugs her name into the Yahoo search engine, the result is a blank page.[13]

This puts the burden on Facebook to prove to a European Commission authority that my friend's publication of my embarrassing picture is a legitimate journalistic (or literary or artistic) exercise.

Finally, there is Fleischer's third category of takedown requests: "If someone else posts something about me, do I have a right to delete it?" This, of course, raises the most serious concerns about free expression. The U.S. Supreme Court has held that states cannot pass laws restricting the media from disseminating truthful but embarrassing information—such as the name of a rape victim—as long as the information was legally acquired.[14]

The proposed European regulation, however, treats takedown requests for truthful information posted by others identically to takedown requests for photos I've posted myself that have then been copied by others: both are included in the definition of personal data as "any information relating" to me, regardless of its source.[15] I can demand takedown and the burden, once again, is on the third party to prove that it falls within the exception for journalistic, artistic, or literary exception. This could transform Google, for example, into a censor-in-chief for the European Union, rather than a neutral platform. And because this is a role Google won't want to play, it may instead produce blank pages whenever a European user types in the name of someone who has objected to a nasty blog post or status update.

13. Vinod Sreeharsha, *Google and Yahoo Win Appeal in Argentine Case*, N.Y. Times, Aug. 20, 2010, at B4.
14. Florida Star v. B.J.F., 491 U.S. 524 (1989).
15. Proposed Data Protection Regulation, *supra* note 6, at art 4(2).

It's possible, of course, that although the European regulation defines the right to be forgotten very broadly, it will be applied more narrowly. Europeans have a long tradition of declaring abstract privacy rights in theory that they fail to enforce in practice. And the regulation may be further refined over the next year or so, as the European Parliament and the Council of Ministers hammer out the details. But in announcing the regulation, Reding said she wanted it to be ambiguous so that it could accommodate new technologies in the future. "This regulation needs to stand for 30 years—it needs to be very clear but imprecise enough that changes in the markets or public opinion can be maneuvered in the regulation," she declared ominously.[16] Once the regulation is promulgated, moreover, it will instantly become law throughout the European Union, and if the E.U. withdraws from the safe harbor agreement that is currently in place, the European framework could be imposed on U.S. companies doing business in Europe as well.[17] It's hard to imagine that the Internet that results will be as free and open as it is now.

16. Matt Warman, *EU Fights 'Fierce Lobbying' to Devise Data Privacy Law*, Telegraph (Feb. 9, 2012), *available at* http://www.telegraph.co.uk/technology/internet/9069933/EU-fights-fierce-lobbying-to-devise-data-privacy-law.html.
17. *Private Data, Public Rules*, Economist (Jan. 28, 2012), available at http://www.economist.com/node/21543489.

VIEWPOINT 3

Australia Should Legislate the Right to Sue for Invasion of Privacy

Michael Pearce

In the following viewpoint, Michael Pearce argues that technological change has led to the erosion of privacy in Australia, necessitating legal redress. Pearce contends that protecting the right to privacy is a key feature of democratic societies and that the law needs to reflect that. He calls for the Australian government to pass a law allowing individuals to sue for damages for serious invasions of privacy, as deterrence to misuse of new technologies. Pearce is an Australian lawyer and past president of Liberty Victoria, one of Australia's leading civil liberties organizations.

As you read, consider the following questions:

1. The author expresses concern that smart card technology can violate privacy by recording movements through what three avenues?
2. Whereas Pearce claims that acknowledgement of the right to privacy is a feature of democratic nations, he says it is absent from what kind of states?
3. Drawing an analogy, Pearce says that a right to sue will not eliminate invasions of privacy any more than the law of negligence eliminates what?

Michael Pearce, "Legislate the Right to Privacy," *The Age* (Australia), July 27, 2011.

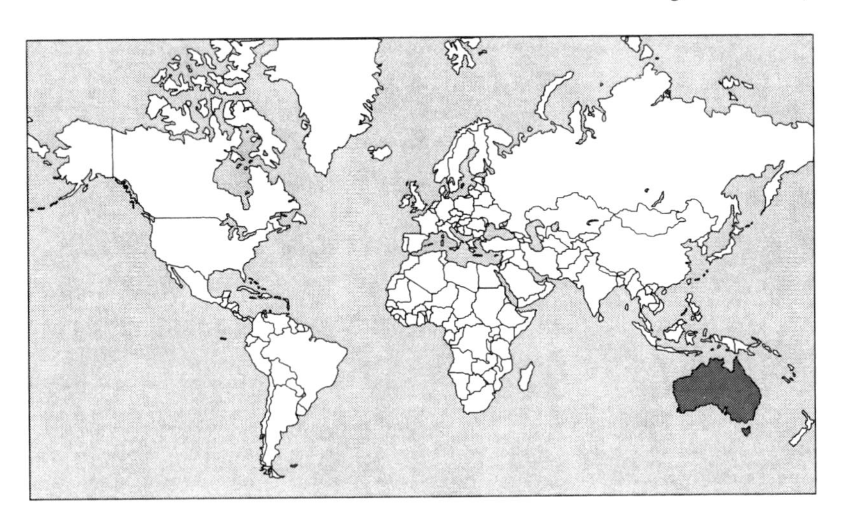

The federal government should be applauded for giving serious consideration to the recommendation of the Australian Law Reform Commission [ALRC] three years ago that Parliament legislate for a right to sue for damages for serious invasion of privacy.

Media companies have sprung to oppose the recommendations. But their arguments are unconvincing.

The Erosion of Privacy

The reasons why Parliament should legislate are more fundamental than the need to respond to the passing wrongdoing of a rogue media company, even if it does control about two-thirds of metropolitan newspaper circulation in this country.

Parliament should act because technological change is eroding privacy to such a degree and so rapidly that, without some legal protection, very little privacy will be left to us before long.

The technological and other innovations that have encroached on privacy in recent years include:

- The Internet, with its capacity to broadcast personal information instantaneously around the world, its spyware to snoop on users and its social networking sites that turn users into open books.

- Mobile phones, with their GPS [Global Positioning System] systems that can track your movements.
- Smart card technology that records your movements (through public transport, toll roads and credit and debit card purchases), profiles your spending habits and your health details.
- The spread of CCTV [closed-circuit television].
- Anti–money laundering legislation that swept away banker-customer confidentiality and compels a range of people from bankers to solicitors to report "suspicious" activities of clients to the government.
- Mandatory reporting legislation that requires health care and other professionals to report suspicions of abuse of various kinds to the government.
- Copying and scanning technology that enables night-club bouncers and taxi drivers to make permanent records of the personal details of their customers.

These innovations no doubt have many positive applications. But they have fundamentally redefined privacy, and it is futile to think we can enjoy the sort of privacy that prevailed before this technology.

Technological change is eroding privacy to such a degree and so rapidly that, without some legal protection, very little privacy will be left to us before long.

The Importance of the Right to Privacy

There are good reasons why we should try to retain as much privacy as possible in the information age.

Privacy can be thought of as denoting that sphere of a person's life that they control completely, to the exclusion of others. What we keep private is a matter of personal choice. The key thing is that choice.

A common feature of democratic societies is the recognition that all citizens are entitled to a private life and to a wide range of choice about what is kept private.

By contrast, the control exercised by totalitarian and authoritarian states is inconsistent with personal privacy. They deny any right to choose to keep things private and permit the state to reach into the deepest recesses of personal lives.

Most of the great human rights instruments marking out the freedoms of democratic societies include a right of privacy: the Universal Declaration of [Human] Rights, the International Covenant on Civil and Political Rights, the EU [European Union] Convention for the Protection of Human Rights and Fundamental Freedoms. The Victorian Charter of Human Rights and Responsibilities recognises a right of privacy.

But the Victorian charter gives only limited legal recognition to this right. It merely requires courts to interpret other legislation in a manner consistent with the right and requires public officials to act in accordance with it.

The Need for Legal Redress of Privacy Violations

There is a patchwork of laws in Australia that requires government agencies and certain other bodies to deal properly with personal information but none of them gives redress of the kind proposed by the Law Reform Commission, i.e., a general right to sue for damages for a serious and intentional invasion of privacy.

Strict regimes for the protection of databases have not managed to defeat human inquisitiveness, leading to a number of serious breaches of privacy in Australia and overseas, quite apart from the recent News Corporation scandal.

In the aftermath of one such breach in the United Kingdom, the motoring journalist Jeremy Clarkson derided the alarm expressed about the disclosure of personal bank account details. He published his own bank account details and was then embarrassed when a hacker accessed his account and transferred £500 to a charity!

Just as the law of negligence developed in response to changing technology and social conditions of the early 20th century, a similar legal development is needed now in the early 21st century.

Clarkson had the sense and good grace to admit he was wrong to be blasé about privacy.

Let us hope the naysayers in Australia can learn the same lesson but less painfully. They should recognise the many and far-reaching intrusions into privacy wrought by recent technological and other innovations. They should acknowledge the need to provide some legal redress for serious breaches of privacy, even if it means less celebrity gossip in the press.

Such a right will no more prevent invasions of privacy than the law of negligence prevents car accidents. But it should serve to reduce them and to provide legal redress in cases of serious personal harm. Just as the law of negligence developed in response to changing technology and social conditions of the early 20th century, a similar legal development is needed now in the early 21st century.

There are serious restrictions on the equitable action for breach of confidence, which prevents it from developing to fill this gap. A legislative response is therefore the best solution. And so the ALRC's recommendation deserves serious consideration and support. The self-interested complaints of media organisations should not drown out the important policy issues behind this proposed reform.

VIEWPOINT 4

Police Surveillance in the United Kingdom Has Gone Too Far

Olly Zanetti

In the following viewpoint, Olly Zanetti argues that the tactics used by the Forward Intelligence Team (FIT) are a violation of the privacy rights of protestors. Zanetti claims that Great Britain should follow New York City's lead by only allowing surveillance when there is reason to think a crime is about to be committed. He contends there is evidence that surveillance is being used to unlawfully build a database of innocent protestors, and he concludes that police files should only be kept for criminals. Zanetti is a journalist and climate change activist.

As you read, consider the following questions:

1. According to the author, what kind of right to privacy exists in public?
2. In what year were guidelines on police surveillance created in New York City, according to Zanetti?
3. According to the author, what evidence was found by a photojournalist to support belief in the existence of a database of protestors?

Olly Zanetti, "You Are Being Watched," *New Internationalist*, vol. 423, June 2009, pp. 21–24.

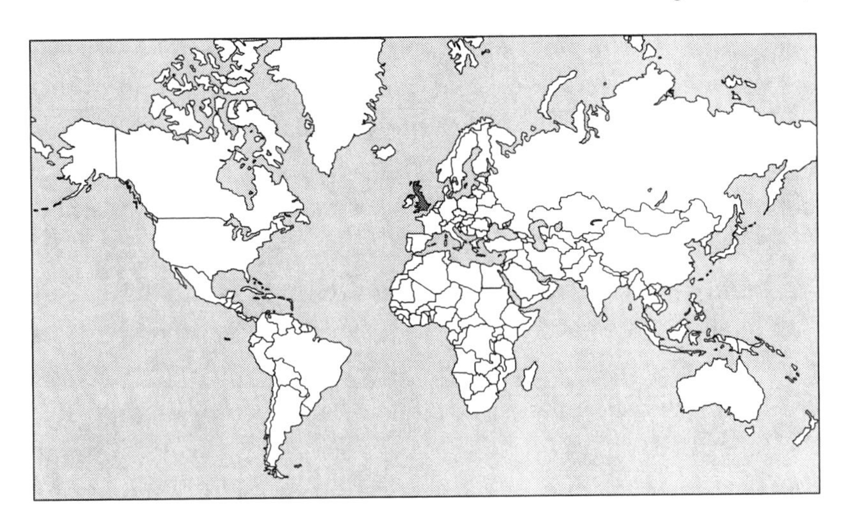

Standing on a makeshift stage at the Climate Camp entrance, two women sing to the cameras that have been trained on them and other campaigners since the event began. Like Climate Camps across the world, 2008's action in Kent, England, took place in the centre of the media's glare. But it wasn't a news crew these activists were singing to. Rather, the serenade was addressed to police photographers from the Forward Intelligence Team: 'the FIT', as they have come to be known.

The Forward Intelligence Team

The FIT's interest extends from demonstrations to the backroom planning meetings of local activist groups. They are at the forefront of a new wave of intimidatory and disproportionate policing and surveillance practices aimed largely, it seems, at cataloguing and riling nonviolent protesters. Set up by Metropolitan Police [Service] Inspector Barry Norman and Sergeant Andy Brittan, the FIT gained notoriety in 1995. The pair attended Reclaim the Streets actions, filmed demonstrators, and attempted to engage them in dialogue, borrowing tactics from the monitoring of football hooliganism in the early 1990s.

Armed with upmarket cameras and camcorders, officers overtly record everything and everyone in their sights. They have even been known to quote their surveillance findings back at activists. 'We know what you're up to,' seems to be the FIT message—the act of data gathering remade as a method of control.

Indeed, the results of FIT surveillance, and so-called intelligence-led policing, hit the headlines recently when, in the early hours of 14 April [2009], 114 activists were preemptively arrested for allegedly conspiring to commit criminal damage and aggravated trespass in a demonstration at Ratcliffe-on-Soar coal-fired power station. This preemptive policing raises serious civil liberties concerns, as Shami Chakrabarti, director of Liberty, notes. 'In the light of the policing of the G20 protests, people up and down the country will want to be confident that there was evidence of a real conspiracy to commit criminal damage by those arrested and that this was not just an attempt by the police to disrupt perfectly legitimate protest.'

So why sing at them? 'It's the only way to deal with it,' says Amelia Gregory, one of the Climate Camp songsters. 'We were there on the gate to welcome people into the camp, people who were being intimidated [by the police], who'd possibly never had this experience before. We had to make them feel comfortable, to make light of it.'

The Right to Privacy in Public

Civil liberties and the right to privacy have become big issues in Britain. We live in a time of unprecedented surveillance by state powers, and of particular interest to them are those who challenge the status quo. Although gathering data on dissent is nothing new, today's technological advances and sheer audacity have moved evidence-gathering techniques up a notch.

In 2005 the *Financial Times* reported that mobile phones could be used as roving bugs, with software remotely activating microphones and transmitting data. Since then, removing batteries and SIM cards from phones before sensitive meetings has become standard practice among activists. And, if recent experience from New Zealand/Aotearoa is anything to go by, even those you hold closest might not be trustworthy. Helping her boyfriend Rob Gilchrist fix his computer, Rochelle Rees, an animal rights campaigner from Christchurch, discovered e-mails which showed he was a police informant—part of a 10-year surveillance operation which went as high as the government's Special Investigations Unit.

There is nothing undercover about the FIT's methods, however. 'Overt filming is a tactic used to combat crime and gather intelligence and evidence,' reads a 2008 Metropolitan Police Authority briefing paper. 'Cameras should be deployed overtly with the staff operating them clearly identifiable as police officers or police staff. The intention of overt filming is to provide reassurance and to reduce the fear of crime as well as to assist in its prevention and detection.'

Civil liberties and the right to privacy have become big issues in Britain.

In May 2008, the FIT hit the headlines when it was revealed that a police force in Essex had decided to use overt filming against alleged troublemakers in the area. Code-named Operation Leopard, officers 'harassed', in the approving words of Home Secretary Jacqui Smith, young people on estates in the county. 'I want police and local agencies to focus on them by giving them a taste of their own medicine,' she explained, while justifying an extension of the tactic to elsewhere in the country. 'Daily visits, repeated warnings and relentless filming of offenders [will occur] to create an environment where there is nowhere to hide.' The targets of Operation Leopard were those known by the police for their persistent misbehaviour.

As the tactic was rolled out, however, it became less directed, with young people stopped, searched and photographed seemingly at random.

'I was absolutely horrified the first time I was FIT-ed,' explains Marina Pepper from the campaign groups Climate Rush and G20 Meltdown. 'I was at Climate Camp. It was dark, I was pushed up against the wall and they took my photograph. I was just going about my business. It was completely designed to intimidate.' As well as targeting individuals, FIT officers target specific events. Before an Earth First meeting at a social club in Brighton, officers snapped everyone entering the building with a long-lens camera. As commentators, including the area's MP [member of Parliament] David Lepper have suggested, this was designed to discourage people from attending, and intimidate those who did.

There is no right to privacy in a public space, so the police—and public—are entitled to record at will.

The FIT's techniques occupy a subtle niche in UK [United Kingdom] law. There is no right to privacy in a public space, so the police—and public—are entitled to record at will. In 2008, this was tested by judicial review. Leaving a shareholders' meeting of the academic publisher and then-arms-fair-organizer Reed Elsevier, Andrew Wood, press officer for the group Campaign Against Arms Trade, was photographed. He applied for the review on the grounds that this photography was in contravention of his human rights. Articles of the European Convention [on Human Rights] which govern the right to privacy and the right to freedom of political expression were cited.

The review found no contravention had occurred. Referring to the case of photographs taken of model Naomi Campbell leaving a drug therapy centre, in which it was stated that '[t]he famous and even the not-so-famous who go out in public must accept that they may be photographed without their consent', the judge ruled there had been no undue interference with Wood's right to privacy. Likewise, under articles governing freedom of political expression, the judge decided that the recording of images in no way inhibited the claimant's political activity.

The Handschu Guidelines

This police tactic is not unique to Britain. However, under an extraordinary agreement, activists in New York—where it was also used—have won the right to maintain their privacy. Under what are called the Handschu guidelines, tight controls are placed on the type of evidence gathering police may undertake on individuals and the groups with which they affiliate. Following extensive and intrusive data gathering by the New York City Police Department (NYPD) intelligence team in the 1950s and 1960s, a class action lawsuit was brought in 1971 against the police in which political activist and lawyer Barbara Ellen Handschu was the main plaintiff.

The guidelines, which were finalized in 1985, placed strict controls on the methods and type of covert surveillance that police were permitted to undertake, and required a detailed paper trail to be created should surveillance occur. 'Most broadly, and probably most importantly,' explains Arthur Eisenberg, legal director of the New York Civil Liberties Union (NYCLU), 'the settlement prohibited police from engaging in surveillance resulting in the creation of a police file, unless there was evidence that a crime had been committed or was about to be committed.' This rule effectively outlawed widespread police photography.

After functioning with reasonable success through the 1980s and 1990s, the conservative Mayor [Michael] Bloomberg, citing terrorism concerns, arranged with Judge [Charles S.] Haight, overseer in the original Handschu case, to modify much of the agreement. In 2004 new regulations were issued by the NYPD, which allowed 'the use of photographic or video equipment by operational personnel to accurately record police operations or other public activity if a permissible operational objective exists'. The scope was massive, given that an 'operational objective' was defined as any time when, at a public event, 'accurate documentation is deemed potentially beneficial or useful'.

While in spirit the Handschu agreement protects little not covered by the Constitution's First Amendment (which upholds freedom of speech, freedom of assembly and the right 'to petition the Government for a redress of grievances'), in practice Eisenberg believes it proved significant. 'Going back a number of years, decisions have been made by the Supreme Court which severely weaken First Amendment rights in this context. [They] have made it unenforceable because of what the court has called a "lack of standing", as no individual has been able to show that they are harmed by such intelligence collection. Handschu affords protection beyond that which the First protects.'

Though surveillance officers are still seen on the sidelines of New York demonstrations, they are prohibited from raising their cameras unless they have reason to believe a crime may be about to be committed.

The NYCLU were not going to allow Handschu to be watered down without a fight. So, in April 2007, the police department, Eisenberg and Judge Haight were back in court to discuss the matter. Though the police department argued that the agreement should remain in its attenuated form, the debate was in fact academic, because two weeks earlier, police officials had surreptitiously scrapped it.

It was not until September 2008 that Eisenberg and his colleagues were made aware of this. For 18 months, they had been working on legal proceedings to overturn a ruling the police had already revoked.

'It's quite remarkable,' said Eisenberg. 'I don't know whether it was a case of the right hand not telling the left what it was doing, or whether there was some more malevolent goal. There may well have been.' It has been speculated that this was a case of the police cutting their losses. The *New York Times* had run an investigative piece into the NYPD's surveillance tactics. That the tactics were then dropped perhaps indicated the department's fear of further bad press. Though surveillance officers are still seen on the sidelines of New York demonstrations, they are prohibited from raising their cameras unless they have reason to believe a crime may be about to be committed.

Turning the Tables on Surveillance

The UK legal system has been unwilling to order similar restraint from police intelligence units, yet the FIT has not gone un-resisted. In April 2007, Val Swain was attending a widely advertised activist meeting. Shortly before it began, around 10 FIT officers arrived. Their photographer took pictures of everyone entering the building, both campaigners and, because the meeting was held in the University of London Union, students unconnected with the discussion.

The week before, Swain had been at another meeting at which FIT officers had been similarly deployed. 'I decided that I could not continue being active politically under these conditions. I would either have to stop going to meetings, or I would have to do something about it.' She chose the latter. When the officers refused to stop filming, she held up a banner she had already prepared, on which she had written 'protect our privacy', to obstruct the FIT cameras.

The officers pushed her away, then 'violently arrested' her for allegedly obstructing a police officer in his duty. In court Swain argued that the police were breaching privacy rights, and did not have authority to use force to get their pictures. However, she says, 'the judge decided to dodge the whole

"Big Brother," cartoon by Kjell Nilsson-Maki, www.CartoonStock.com. Copyright © by Kjell Nilsson-Maki. Reproduction rights obtainable from www.CartoonStock.com. Reproduced by permission.

issue'. Because the photographer was freelance and not a serving police officer, he decided that the charges could not stand, therefore refusing to enter into the wider debate.

That direct action marked the beginning of the group Fitwatch. As well as using banners, potential Fitwatchers are advised to play officers at their own game, following them, listening in to their conversations, and taking their photographs. Information gleaned is made publicly available online. As

Emily Apple from Fitwatch notes, psychologically it was not an easy movement to start. 'We felt any reaction to the police detracted from the subject we were protesting about. But as it progressed, what we did on the street was pretty much ineffective because of the way they were policing. So tackling the FIT seemed necessary.'

Since Swain's case, several others have been brought against Fitwatchers. While most have been acquitted, five were recently convicted of obstructing the police. They have lodged an appeal, but new evidence has come to light and the appeal has been put on hold.

Common sense dictates that these photographs are being taken by the police to be used for something.

The Existence of a Database

That new evidence relates to the earlier judicial review brought by Andrew Wood. During proceedings, the Metropolitan Police's legal team explicitly noted that there was no invasion of privacy through overt photography because it 'was not an exercise in compiling any national database'. Yet in a Fitwatch trial, PC [Police Chief] Dan Collins admitted that a database was being assembled. An investigation by the *Guardian* newspaper in March 2009 recorded a similar admission by a senior officer, providing further proof. Photographs and video footage are being retained electronically, the *Guardian* suggested. It also suggested that names are being associated with photographs, and a database is being prepared which contains details of many thousands of protesters, irrespective of whether they have broken the law.

Additional evidence of the existence of such a database came from photojournalist Marc Vallée. When FIT officers attend demonstrations, they are issued with cards, called 'spotter's cards', on which the faces of activists they wish to track are printed. 'I was working at a protest against the attack on Gaza. I saw an officer with a camera speaking to another officer, who I know works with the FIT. They were going through a notebook which had a number of pictures in it, spotter's cards. And I got a shot of it. Enlarging the picture, you can see the mug shots with people's names underneath each one. Not codes or aliases, but full names. They were clearly looking for particular individuals.'

On the existence of the database, campaigners are frank. 'It wasn't a surprise, I think it was fairly common knowledge amongst activists,' said Amelia Gregory. Common sense dictates that these photographs are being taken by the police to be used for something. Anecdotal evidence backs this up. When Marina Pepper arrived at an action, she was quizzed by a FIT officer on a matter from her personal life she had told few friends about, but had mentioned once on the front line of a protest. 'I asked him how he knew that. "I just guessed," he told me.' In spite of this overwhelming evidence, a police press release insisted that 'the Met Police Public Order branch does not hold a database of protesters'.

The Targeting of Journalists

As Vallée's experience has shown, the FIT's interest is not limited to activists. Though a press-card-carrying member of the media, he has been subjected to significant harassment. After recording images of a particularly brutal arrest at the 2008 Climate Camp, he and colleagues went to a nearby restaurant to file footage using their Wi-Fi connection.

'There were six of us, all of whom held press cards,' Vallée explains. 'We had laptops open, cameras all around, and were uploading images. Then a colleague said: "look behind you, out the window." And there was an evidence-gathering crew filming us doing our job. That was very concerning. There was no legitimate reason for them to be doing that. If the state, through the police, are building up a list of which media organizations and journalists have covered particular events, they may in the future attempt to get hold of the material we've collected. It's speculation, but it's the only reason I or the National Union of Journalists [NUJ] can think of.'

In May 2008 Jeremy Dear, general secretary of the NUJ, wrote to the Home Secretary: 'The routine and deliberate targeting of photographers and other journalists by the FIT undermines media freedom and can serve to intimidate photographers trying to carry out their lawful work. The rights of photographers to work free from threat, harassment and intimidation must be upheld.' These concerns were echoed in a recent report by the parliamentary Joint Committee on Human Rights.

With calls for change coming not just from activists, but from establishment figures too, the era of panoptical surveillance and 'harassment' policing should have had its day. Whether Britain, or indeed any other country where similar tactics are deployed, will follow New York's lead is another matter. What is clear is the need for a strict message from the top. Police files are for criminals, while legitimate protest is just that. Legitimate.

VIEWPOINT 5

The Right to Privacy in India Is Threatened by Rigid Codes of Morality

Siddharth Narrain

In the following viewpoint, Siddharth Narrain argues that there are many examples where the right to privacy of individuals has been violated due to regulations that allow law enforcement to uphold morality. However, Narrain points to a recent court case that not only decriminalized homosexuality, but also said that the privacy rights of individuals may not be violated in an attempt to defend public morality. He concludes that the right to privacy should be protected in India using this reasoning. Narrain is a member of the Alternative Law Forum in Bangalore, India.

As you read, consider the following questions:

1. According to Narrain, Irfan Khan was suspended from his university job on what grounds?
2. According to the author, a recent case in the Delhi High Court linked the right to privacy with what other right?
3. The right to free speech in India is qualified by what restriction, according to Narrain?

Siddharth Narrain, "Sex, Lies, and Videotape: The Right to Privacy in India," *Infochange*, March 2010. Reproduced by permission.

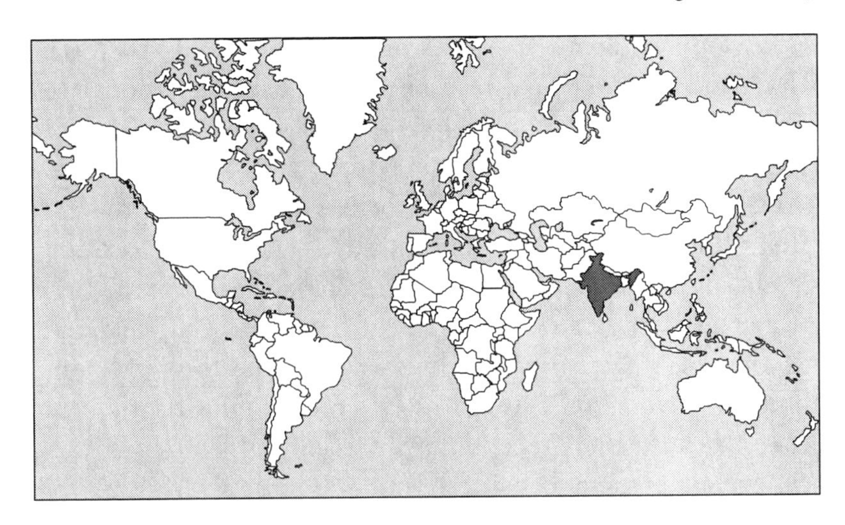

The discourse over privacy in India has been circumscribed by views on morality and what is seen as acceptable to Indian morals and values. Two recent incidents illustrate the complexities of this debate.

Two Recent Incidents

The first is the widely publicised suspension of Professor S.R. Siras, who was a Reader in the Department of Modern Indian Languages at the Aligarh Muslim University (AMU). Sixty-four-year-old Siras had taught for nearly 20 years at AMU, and was on the verge of retirement. The professor was with a friend (who was an autorickshaw driver) within the confines of his home when three men suddenly appeared from the next room and forcibly photographed Professor Siras, claiming they were from the press. Within a few minutes of this, a group of officials from AMU entered the house. This group included the proctor, media adviser and public relations officer of AMU, clearly showing that this was a setup in which the AMU authorities were involved. Those who have been following events within AMU are not surprised by this incident. AMU has instituted a moral police force called the 'Local Intelligence Unit' that is paid to keep tabs on students and teachers.

In January 2010, an AMU research scholar, Irfan Khan, who was in a consensual relationship with Asma Firdous, was suspended from the university on grounds of 'moral turpitude, intimidation and assault'. Though Irfan Khan and Asma Firdous had got married a day before the filing of the FIR [first information report], the university authorities chose to go ahead and suspend him. Irfan and Asma approached the Allahabad High Court, which ruled that both Irfan Khan and his wife had married out of free will. Despite this, AMU authorities have refused to withdraw the suspension of Irfan Khan, because they believe that marrying of one's own free will against parental consent amounts to moral turpitude and violates the moral code set by the AMU authorities.

The discourse over privacy in India has been circumscribed by views on morality and what is seen as acceptable to Indian morals and values.

The Issue of Privacy

Ironically, the incident involving Professor Siras took place a few months after the Delhi High Court decriminalised homosexuality in India and talked at length about both the right to dignity and the right to privacy of lesbian, gay, bisexual and transgender [LGBT] persons. The Delhi High Court, in its judgment quoted the South African Constitutional Court: "The right to privacy recognises that we all have a sphere of private intimacy and autonomy which allows us to establish and nurture human relationships without interference from the outside community. The way in which one gives expression to one's sexuality is at the core of this area of private intimacy. If, in expressing one's sexuality, one acts consensually and without harming the other, invasion of that precinct will be a breach of privacy." The high court, in its widely discussed judgment, not only affirmed the right of same-sex partners to have consensual sex within the privacy of their home, but also went on to affirm 'decisional' privacy of LGBT persons, linking their right to privacy to the right to autonomy and sexuality.

While the debate around the AMU action was framed as one of homophobia and moral policing, the question of the right to privacy is an important element in this discussion. When a state-funded university has persons on its payroll to snoop on and watch students and faculty, it reflects poorly on the culture of instituted moral policing and the complete disregard for the right to privacy of the large community of students and teachers there.

The second incident, which involved very different circumstances, is the case of Swami Paramahamsa Nithyananda, allegedly caught on camera in a 'compromising' position with Tamil actress Ranjitha. While there are a number of theories circulating about who planned this expose, it was clearly done without his knowledge. While the controversy in this case may have to do with the swami's public face as a man of God and the faith that a large number of persons have placed in his divinity, it does not take away from the fact that his privacy was violated. Such was the fury that erupted after the tapes were played on Sun TV, that the actress had to go into hiding and his ashram was attacked by a mob.

The Right to Privacy in Indian Law

The broader right to privacy has evolved from being a tort law to an integral part of article 21 jurisprudence. In the Kharak Singh and Gobind Singh cases, the Supreme Court was deciding on the validity of regulations that allowed domiciliary visits by the police. It held that the right to privacy derives from an English common law maxim which asserts that "Every man's house is his castle". The majority of judges in this case located 'privacy' as an aspect of the right to liberty protected under article 21 of the Constitution. However, the boundaries of the legally protected right to privacy seem to dissolve when

The Right to Privacy in India

In India, as in the United Kingdom, there is no tort of privacy. India's law of torts (that is, civil wrongs punishable in damages) is based on case law, English and foreign. However, the Supreme Court of India has inferred right to privacy from the ones explicitly guaranteed. Article 21 of the Constitution contains a guarantee of personal liberty, and it is obvious that personal liberty also involves the right to privacy.

A.G. Noorani, "A Case for Privacy,"
Frontline *(India), November 19–December 2, 2011.*

the violation of the right is seen through the lens of moral turpitude. Legal researcher Saptarshi Mandal, in a recent piece, has pointed out that the analytical framework developed by the courts in India is insufficient to explain how criminal law views privacy in regulating sex. Thus, while the state intervenes in cases of adultery to protect sexual access to the wife from third-party interference, in cases of marital rape the state will not intervene. Law protects only what is considered 'legitimate' private sex, i.e., sex within marriage.

The high court has clearly said that the right to liberty, dignity and privacy of individuals cannot be restrained based on the notion of 'public morality'.

An example of how these rigid codes of morality play out was the controversy over Tamil actress Khushboo's statements relating to premarital sex, in 2005. Khushboo, in an interview to the newsmagazine *India Today*, said that it was all right for girls to have premarital sex as long as they took care to avoid unwanted pregnancies and sexually transmitted diseases. These comments were carried in a Tamil magazine and created a storm in Tamil Nadu. Twenty-three cases related to obscenity and defamation were filed against her, and she was slammed by most of her fellow actors and political parties in Tamil Nadu. She was forced to apologise for her remarks.

Besides laws like the obscenity law and section 377 of the Indian penal code (the law that until recently criminalised homosexuality), which are premised on a certain conservative morality inherited from British times, a number of laws in India have the word 'morality' inbuilt in their very provisions. For instance, contract law (section 23 of the Indian Contract Act) declares contracts that have an "immoral object" to be void. This is one of the provisions used to stigmatise sex workers. Draconian legislations like the provisions of the Immoral Traffic (Prevention) Act (IPTA) that allow for search without warrants have been held to be constitutional by Indian courts since "future cohabitation" is declared immoral. Thus, in sex work (and until recently in homosexual sex) the private nature of the sexual act was considered irrelevant. The right to free speech under article 21 is qualified by reasonable restrictions, one of which is 'public morality'. This provision has been used by the Supreme Court to uphold provisions of the Cinematograph Act that justify pre-censorship of cinema.

By making a distinction between "constitutional" and "public morality", the Delhi High Court has provided one route through which the 'morality' argument could be circumvented. The high court has clearly said that the right to liberty, dignity and privacy of individuals cannot be restrained based on the notion of 'public morality'. The court has based its view of constitutional morality on liberal democratic ideals underlining the Indian Constitution. It remains to be seen if this logic is used constructively by other courts and in public discourse to protect the right to privacy of individuals like Professor Siras and Swami Nithyananda.

VIEWPOINT 6

In China, the Demand for Greater Privacy Rights Is Growing

Peter Foster

In the following viewpoint, Peter Foster argues that the Chinese are demanding more respect for their right to privacy, in conjunction with an overall growing awareness and assertion of individual rights. Foster contends that although the government in China severely limits the right to privacy, he claims that the Chinese people are pushing back for greater rights and are having some success with government authorities. Foster is the Telegraph's *US editor based in Washington, DC. He moved to America in January 2012 after three years based in Beijing.*

As you read, consider the following questions:

1. According to the author, what do the reactions to surveillance by the Chinese illustrate about individual rights?
2. The Chinese have no right to privacy when it conflicts with what, according to Foster?
3. What knowledge do Chinese citizens use to assume greater rights, according to the author?

Peter Foster, "China's Bugged Taxis and the Right to Privacy," *Telegraph* (UK), September 22, 2010. blogs.telegraph.co.uk.

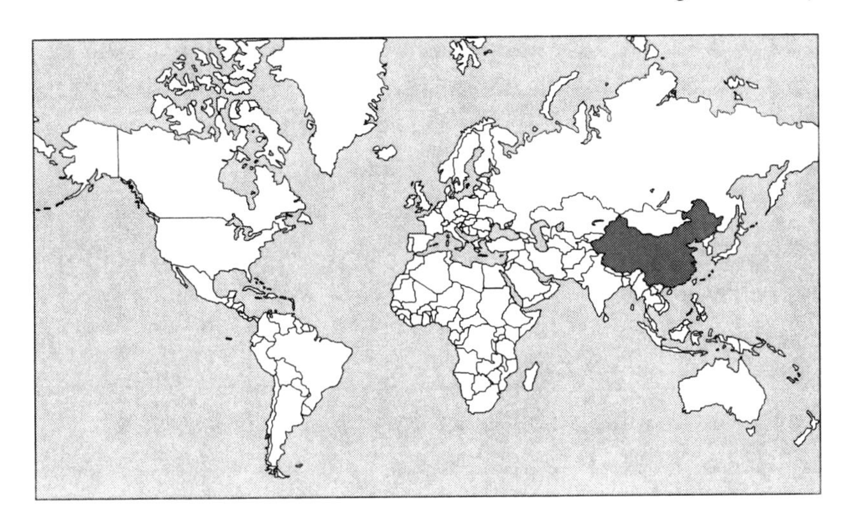

I've been away travelling in Cambodia and southern China on two longer-term projects.

Chinese Reaction to Surveillance

Back in Beijing an article in the *Global Times* about 'bugging'—i.e., the installation of voice and video recorders—in taxis in Chongqing, Xi'an, Beijing and Wuhu immediately caught my eye this morning [September 22, 2010].

Not so much for the fact itself—as the piece neatly points out, quoting a British resident of Beijing, we Brits are no strangers to surveillance by the state—but for the reaction of ordinary Chinese people to the decision.

"It makes me uncomfortable. I feel like I'm being watched all the time," local resident Han Yun told China's Xinhua News Agency, echoing a common thread in the cities concerned that the cameras are a violation of privacy.

Global Times, rather melodramatically for my money, quotes a 24-year-old Beijing civil servant as saying that he doesn't say a word in the taxi—not to the driver, his wife or his mobile phone—for fear of revealing something he shouldn't.

"It feels like I'm under surveillance when I'm inside the taxi. There is always a device recording what I'm saying," he says, "I choose to stay silent because I do not want to reveal any personal information in the taxi."

The reactions speak of a growing awareness about individual rights in China which, as much as any reform in the law itself, is forcing the state to change its behavior.

The Right to Privacy

There was another example in the papers only last week.

China is currently preparing for a census which is causing similar ripples because of people being wary of disclosing financial information (i.e., just how many houses they own thanks to their grey and black income) or whether they have more children than they should under the one-child policy.

One official recently reported that he'd had a terrible time getting people to sign the forms, observing that the last time China did a census, officials just walked into people's houses and demanded to see their papers.

Not any more, he said, (ruefully, perhaps)—"people know their rights".

Of course, 'rights' is a tricky concept in China, since the law is weak and the [Communist] Party can (and frequently does) overrule constitutional and legal rights in the name of protecting 'social harmony' or its fundamental right to rule, which in its view, comes down to the same thing.

China's citizens do increasingly have and demand rights.

In theory, according to Feng Yujun, a law professor at the Renmin University of China quoted by *Global Times*, Chinese citizens actually don't have any 'right to privacy'—especially when it conflicts with the 'public' interest (or Party interest, again the same thing).

"The concept of privacy was not written into the general provisions of the civil law when it was issued in 1986," he said, "which makes it hard for the public to protect their privacy through the legal process."

The Demand for Greater Rights

In practice, however, China's citizens do increasingly have and demand rights.

They are not codified in law (which is the problem in cases of last resort) but born out of a process of pushing and pulling that is constantly going on between the citizens and the government with the citizens winning ground for themselves inch by inch.

Even without the law to support them, China citizens know that the governing authorities are conscious of how far people are prepared to tolerate having their rights ignored or abused, and they use that knowledge collectively to gradually assume greater rights to themselves.

You read, and I often write, about the arbitrary abuse of rights in China by the police, by corrupt officials, by government and the courts but these need to be seen as markers along a long, winding road that is—even with periodic switchbacks and U-turns—heading in the general direction of greater freedom.

Periodical and Internet Sources Bibliography

The following articles have been selected to supplement the diverse views presented in this chapter.

Chris Berg	"Internet Laws a Sledgehammer Approach to Privacy," *Sydney Morning Herald*, February 12, 2012.
Peter Bright	"Europe Proposes a 'Right to Be Forgotten,'" Ars Technica, January 25, 2012. http://arstechnica.com.
John Hendel	"Why Journalists Shouldn't Fear Europe's 'Right to Be Forgotten,'" *Atlantic*, January 25, 2012.
Human Rights Watch	"'The Root of Humiliation': Abusive Identity Checks in France," January 2012. www.hrw.org.
Manasi Kakatkar-Kulkarni	"Essential Surveillance and the Right to Privacy," Foreign Policy Association, April 28, 2010. http://foreignpolicyblogs.com.
Tessa Mayes	"We Have No Right to Be Forgotten Online," *Guardian* (UK), March 18, 2011.
Osita Mba	"Pride and Prejudice: How Not to Fight Homophobia in Africa," *New Statesman*, June 2, 2010.
Helen Pidd	"Facebook Facial Recognition Software Violates Privacy Laws, Says Germany," *Guardian* (UK), August 3, 2011.
Geoffrey Wheatcroft	"Privacy, Libel and the Case of Dominique Strauss-Kahn," *National Interest*, May 19, 2011.
Patricia J. Williams	"Do We Have Any Right to Privacy Outside Our Homes?," *Nation*, December 12, 2011.

For Further Discussion

Chapter 1

1. Yasmin Alibhai-Brown claims that speech can incite hatred, which eventually leads to violence. Do you think Robert Skidelsky would agree that sometimes such speech is harmful enough to prevent? Anchor your discussion in a particular example.
2. Jillian Kestler-D'Amours argues that Palestine advocates on university campuses should be allowed to protest in events such as Israeli Apartheid Week, whereas Avi Benlolo calls for an end to the event. When, if ever, do you think speech should be rightfully disallowed based on its hatefulness? Explain your reasoning.

Chapter 2

1. Based on the viewpoints in this chapter, what similarities are there among countries that have limited media freedom? What conclusions might be drawn from the correlation? Use examples from the text to support your answer.

Chapter 3

1. According to the viewpoint by Mordechai Kremnitzer and Lina Saba and the viewpoint by Kenneth Roth, what practice do both Israel and the United States engage in that denies due process?
2. Describe how the need for security is used to justify a restriction of rights for terrorism suspects in at least two of the countries mentioned in this chapter.

Chapter 4

1. Referencing at least three viewpoints in this chapter, illustrate how the right to privacy comes in conflict with other values. Attempt to explain how the conflict should be resolved.

Organizations to Contact

The editors have compiled the following list of organizations concerned with the issues debated in this book. The descriptions are derived from materials provided by the organizations. All have publications or information available for interested readers. The list was compiled on the date of publication of the present volume; the information provided here may change. Be aware that many organizations take several weeks or longer to respond to inquiries, so allow as much time as possible.

African Commission on Human and Peoples' Rights
31 Bijilo Annex Layout, Kombo North District
Western Region, PO Box 673, Banjul
Gambia
(220) 441 0505 • fax: (220) 441 0504
e-mail: au-banjul@africa-union.org
website: www.achpr.org

The African Commission on Human and Peoples' Rights interprets the African Charter on Human and Peoples' Rights, aiming to promote and protect the rights of Africans. The commission undertakes studies and research on African human rights; organizes seminars, symposia, and conferences; disseminates information; and makes recommendations to African governments. Available at its website is the text of the African Charter on Human and Peoples' Rights, which includes the protection of several civil liberties.

American Civil Liberties Union (ACLU)
125 Broad Street, 18th Floor, New York, NY 10004
(212) 549-2500
e-mail: infoaclu@aclu.org
website: www.aclu.org

The American Civil Liberties Union (ACLU) is a national organization that works to defend Americans' civil rights as guaranteed in the US Constitution. The ACLU works in courts, legislatures, and communities to defend First Amendment rights, the right to equal protection, the right to due process, and the right to privacy. The ACLU publishes the semiannual newsletter *Civil Liberties Alert*, as well as briefing papers, including the report "Locking Up Our Children."

Amnesty International
1 Easton Street, London WC1X 0DW
United Kingdom
(44) 20 7413 5500 • fax: (44) 20 7956 1157
website: www.amnesty.org

Amnesty International is a worldwide movement of people who campaign for internationally recognized human rights for all. Amnesty International conducts research and generates action to prevent and end grave abuses of human rights and to demand justice for those whose rights have been violated. At its website, Amnesty International has numerous publications on a variety of human rights issues, including detention and imprisonment.

Article 19
Free Word Centre, 60 Farringdon Road, London EC1R 3GA
(44) 20 7324 2500 • fax: (44) 20 7490 0566
e-mail: info@article19.org
website: www.article19.org

Article 19 works to protect freedom of expression, including freedom of information, as a fundamental human right that is also central to the protection of other rights. With offices throughout the world, Article 19 fights for all hostages of censorship, defends dissenting voices, and campaigns against laws and practices that silence. Article 19 publishes statements and advocacy letters, as well as reports such as "Middle East and North Africa: Historic Opportunity for Freedom of Expression."

Committee to Protect Journalists (CPJ)
330 Seventh Avenue, 11th Floor, New York, NY 10001
(212) 465-1004 • fax: (212) 465-9568

e-mail: info@cpj.org
website: www.cpj.org

The Committee to Protect Journalists (CPJ) is an independent, nonprofit organization that works to promote press freedom worldwide by defending the rights of journalists to report the news without fear of reprisal. CPJ publicly reveals abuses against the press, warns journalists and news organizations where attacks on press freedom are occurring, and organizes vigorous public protests and works through diplomatic channels to effect change. CPJ publishes articles and news releases; special reports; and *Attacks on the Press*, an annual survey of press freedom around the world.

Electronic Frontier Foundation (EFF)

454 Shotwell Street, San Francisco, CA 94110-1914
(415) 436-9333 • fax: (415) 436-9993
e-mail: information@eff.org
website: www.eff.org

The Electronic Frontier Foundation (EFF) works to promote the public interest in critical battles affecting digital rights by defending free speech, privacy, innovation, and consumer rights. EFF provides legal assistance in cases where it believes it can help shape the law. EFF publishes a newsletter and reports such as "New Agreement Between the United States and Europe Will Compromise the Privacy Rights of International Travelers."

Freedom House

1301 Connecticut Avenue NW, Floor 6
Washington, DC 20036
(202) 296-5101 • fax: (202) 293-2840
e-mail: info@freedomhouse.org
website: www.freedomhouse.org

Freedom House is an independent watchdog organization that supports the expansion of freedom around the world. Freedom House supports democratic change, monitors freedom, and advocates for democracy and human rights. Annually, Freedom House publishes the Freedom in the World survey and the Freedom of the Press index.

Human Rights Watch (HRW)

350 Fifth Avenue, 34th Floor, New York, NY 10118-3299
(212) 290-4700 • fax: (212) 736-1300
e-mail: hrwnyc@hrw.org
website: www.hrw.org

Human Rights Watch (HRW) is dedicated to protecting the human rights of people around the world. HRW investigates human rights abuses, educates the public, and works to change policy and practice. Among its numerous publications is the report "Beaten, Blacklisted, and Behind Bars."

International Freedom of Expression Exchange (IFEX)

555 Richmond Street West, Suite 1101, PO Box #407
Toronto, Ontario M5V 3B1
Canada
(416) 515-9622 • fax: (416) 515-7879
e-mail: ifex@ifex.org
website: www.ifex.org

The International Freedom of Expression Exchange (IFEX) is a global network of ninety-five organizations working to defend and promote the right to free expression. IFEX circulates information about free expression to raise awareness, assists members to defend and promote free expression, and facilitates campaigns worldwide. IFEX publishes the weekly *IFEX Digest*, the weekly *IFEX Communiqué*, and other resources, all available at its website.

Liberty

26–30 Strutton Ground, London SW1P 2HR
United Kingdom
(44) 20 7403 3888
website: www.liberty-human-rights.org.uk

Liberty is a non-party membership organization aiming to protect civil liberties and human rights in the United Kingdom. Liberty campaigns to protect basic rights and freedoms through the courts, in Parliament, and in the wider community. Liberty publishes campaign materials, policy papers, fact sheets, articles, and speeches, all available at its website.

National Coalition Against Censorship (NCAC)

19 Fulton Street, Suite 407, New York, NY 10038
(212) 807-6222 • fax: (212) 807-6245
e-mail: ncac@ncac.org
website: www.ncac.org

The National Coalition Against Censorship (NCAC) is an alliance of fifty-two participating organizations dedicated to protecting free expression and access to information. It has many projects dedicated to educating the public and protecting free expression, including the Free Expression Policy Project, the Kids' Right to Read Project, the Knowledge Project: Censorship and Science, and the Youth Free Expression Network. Among its publications is "The First Amendment in Schools."

PEN International

Brownlow House, 50/51 High Holborn, London WC1V 6ER
United Kingdom
(44) 020 7405 0338
e-mail: info@pen-international.org
website: www.pen-international.org

PEN International campaigns on behalf of writers across the globe who are persecuted, harassed, and attacked for what they have written or simply for being a writer. PEN International also runs programs and events celebrating the bond between literature and freedom of expression, believing that one cannot exist meaningfully without the other. PEN International publishes the quarterly literary review *The Magazine*, featuring original work by contemporary writers from around the world.

Reporters Without Borders (Reporters Sans Frontières)
47 Rue Vivienne, 75002 Paris
France
(33) 1 44 83 84 84 • fax: (33) 1 45 23 11 51
e-mail: rsf@rsf.org
website: en.rsf.org

Reporters Without Borders, also known as Reporters Sans Frontières, is an international organization that aims to protect the freedom of the press worldwide. Reporters Without Borders defends journalists who are persecuted for doing their job, fights against censorship, gives aid to media outlets in difficulty, and works to improve the safety of journalists, especially those in war zones. In addition to publishing news from around the world, Reporters Without Borders publishes several reports, including "Media in the Eye of the Storm as Revolutions Sweep the Arab World."

Bibliography of Books

Bruce Ackerman — *Before the Next Attack: Preserving Civil Liberties in an Age of Terrorism.* New Haven, CT: Yale University Press, 2006.

Eric Barendt, ed. — *Freedom of the Press.* Burlington, VT: Ashgate, 2009.

Colin J. Bennett and David Lyon, eds. — *Playing the Identity Card: Surveillance, Security, and Identification in Global Perspective.* New York: Routledge, 2008.

Alison Brysk — *Global Good Samaritans: Human Rights as Foreign Policy.* New York: Oxford University Press, 2009.

Tony Bunyan — *The War on Freedom and Democracy: Essays on Civil Liberties in Europe.* Nottingham, England: Spokesman Books, 2006.

John C. Domino — *Civil Rights and Liberties in the 21st Century.* New York: Longman, 2010.

Stephen M. Feldman — *Free Expression and Democracy in America: A History.* Chicago, IL: University of Chicago Press, 2008.

A.C. Grayling — *Liberty in the Age of Terror: A Defence of Civil Liberties and Enlightenment Values.* London, England: Bloomsbury, 2010.

David H. Holtzman — *Privacy Lost: How Technology Is Endangering Your Privacy*. San Francisco, CA: Jossey-Bass, 2006.

David L. Hudson Jr. — *The Right to Privacy*. New York: Chelsea House, 2010.

Rebecca MacKinnon — *Consent of the Networked: The Worldwide Struggle for Internet Freedom*. New York: Basic Books, 2012.

Jon L. Mills — *Privacy: The Lost Right*. New York: Oxford University Press, 2008.

Peter Navarro and Greg Autry — *Death by China: Confronting the Dragon—A Global Call to Action*. Upper Saddle River, NJ: Prentice Hall, 2011.

Aryeh Neier — *Taking Liberties: Four Decades in the Struggle for Rights*. New York: PublicAffairs, 2003.

Erik Ringmar — *A Blogger's Manifesto: Free Speech and Censorship in the Age of the Internet*. New York: Anthem Press, 2007.

Kartik Sharma et al. — *Freedom of the Press: Using the Law to Defend Journalists*. New Delhi, India: Human Rights Law Network, 2009.

Maria J. Stephan, ed. — *Civilian Jihad: Nonviolent Struggle, Democratization, and Governance in the Middle East*. New York: Palgrave Macmillan, 2009.

Anastassia Tsoukala — *Football Hooliganism in Europe: Security and Civil Liberties in the Balance.* New York: Palgrave Macmillan, 2009.

Robin Tudge — *The No-Nonsense Guide to Global Surveillance.* Oxford, England: New Internationalist, 2011.

Laura Valentini — *Justice in a Globalized World: A Normative Framework.* Oxford, England: Oxford University Press, 2011.

Samantha R. Weber, ed. — *Promoting Global Internet Freedom.* Hauppauge, NY: Nova Science Publishers, 2010.

Index

Geographic headings and page numbers in **boldface** refer to viewpoints about that country or region.

D

E

J

K

L

M

N

R

S

T

U

V

W

X

Y

Z

CPSIA information can be obtained
at www.ICGtesting.com
Printed in the USA
FFOW021855261112